40

HADITH

OF IMAM AN-NAWAWI

الأربعين النووية

Arabic Text With
English Translation

الأربعين النووية

40 HADIT OF IMAM AN-NAWAWI
ISBN: 9798728677352

Table of Contents

Introduction

In the name of Allah, the Entirely Merciful, the Especially Merciful

Imam al-Nawawi's collection of 40 Hadiths is one of the most significant collections of hadiths we have nowadays. Imam al Nawawi in fact gathered a total of 42 hadiths for this collection, not 40. This person was one of the most greatest figures of Islam and lived from 631 A.H. to 676 A.H, died at the age of 45. Allah (Sobhanh wa taala) granted him blessing and prosperity in his work so that he could make magnificent contributions to Islam before deceasing at an early age.

Imam al-Nawawi was a scholar in various different fields of Islamic studies. The massiveness of his works in these different domains is so magnificent that if someone wants to study fiqh, hadith, spirituality, or Quran; one have to pass through Imam al- Nawawi. Among his works with the 40 Hadiths, he authored Al-Adhkar, Riyad al-Saliheen, and commentary of Sahih al-Bukhari and Sahih Muslim.

Imam al-Nawawi starts the "Forty Hadith" with an introduction. Many times we are in the routine of skipping the introduction or rapidly looking through overviews. This is a mistake, particularly when studying Islamic sciences. We have to move forward to a point where we actually know what we know and we can introduce it to others. This is vital so as to able to carry the dawah. In his introduction, Imam al-Nawawi is telling us basically the reason behind the writing of this book, what got him to write this book and this is essential in comprehending the objective of the work.

Points from Imam Al-Nawawi's Introduction

1.) Reason for compilation

Imam al-Nawawi starts by stating a narration related to Prophet Muhammad (Sallat Allh alayhi wa salam) as one reason for the writing of the "Forty Hadith". The hadith point out that anyone who memorizes forty hadiths from the hadiths of the Prophet (Sallat Allh alayhi wa salam), Allah will resurrect him among the scholars. Imam al-Nawawi, however, also obviously states that this hadith is weak.

Types of Hadiths:

This is very significant because we need always know what the source of our data is, whether the hadith is reliable, or not. Is it sahih (authentic), hasan (good)? Or da'if (weak)? and how This assures whether a hadith is acceptable. When it comes to using weak hadiths there is a very essential and deep difference in opinions.

However, Imam al-Nawawi also clearly states that the hadith aforementioned before about memorizing the one who memorizes forty hadiths is not the only cause he is compiling this book, there are other hadith's he quotes that are authentic about seeking and conveying knowledge.

2.) The Criteria of Choosing the Hadiths for this Collection:

Imam al-Nawawi also states there are several people who have transcribed a 40 Hadith collection on different topics, like Zuhd (aestheticism). In this writing however he sought to utilize hadith's that were understandable and cover all areas of religion. They will be short so they can be memorized simply and he made sure that they should be at least acceptable if not entirely authentic.

Imam al-Nawawi flourished in gathering hadith's per his objective. They are very understandable to every single domain of the deen.

Jawami' al-Kalam

The reason why it is so easy to be so comprehensive with only 40 hadith is because the Prophet (Sallah Allah alayhi wa Sallam) was blessed with "jawami' al kalam" (comprehensive speech). The Prophet (Sallah Allah alayhi wa Sallam) says in a hadith,

"I was sent with comprehensive speech."

What this means is as Imam az- Zuhri, one of the great early scholars who died around the turn of first century Hijri said, As far as what has come to us from the understanding of this comprehensive speech the Prophet (Sallah Allah alayhi wa

Sallam) was given, is that Allah gave him the ability to combine many types of ideas that would formally be written in entire books, but the Prophet (Sallah Allah alayhi wa Sallam) could portray in only a couple of sentences.

He (Sallah Allah alayhi wa Sallam) was granted the ability to say simple things that have a myriad of meanings, which is why scholars early on began to compile different sets of hadiths in small amounts to benefit from this quality of the Prophet (Sallah Allah alayhi wa Sallam).

Ibn Salah, one of the first scholars to compile these types of books, has one of the most famous books in hadith sciences called Al-Mukadimah (The Introduction.) He reached up to 26 hadiths with their explanation and then Imam al-Nawawi came and picked up his work. Imam al- Nawawi used the 26 that was explained by Ibn Salah and then added until he finished compiling the 42 hadiths which are today famously known as "Arba'een al-Nawawi," or "Imam Nawawi's Forty Hadith."

عَنْ أَمِيرِ الْمُؤْمِنِينَ أَبِي حَفْصٍ عُمَرَ بْنِ الْخَطَّابِ رَضِيَ اللهُ عَنْهُ قَالَ:

سَمِعْتُ رَسُولَ اللهِ صلى الله عليه وسلم يَقُولُ: " إِنَّمَا الْأَعْمَالُ بِالنِّيَّاتِ، وَإِنَّمَا لِكُلِّ امْرِئٍ مَا نَوَى، فَمَنْ كَانَتْ هِجْرَتُهُ إِلَى اللهِ وَرَسُولِهِ فَهِجْرَتُهُ إِلَى اللهِ وَرَسُولِهِ، وَمَنْ كَانَتْ هِجْرَتُهُ لِدُنْيَا يُصِيبُهَا أَوْ امْرَأَةٍ يَنْكِحُهَا فَهِجْرَتُهُ إِلَى مَا هَاجَرَ إِلَيْهِ".

رَوَاهُ: [الْبُخَارِيُّ] وَ [مُسْلِمٌ].

I. The First Translation

It is narrated on the authority of Amir al-Mu'minin (Leader of the Believers), Abu Hafs 'Umar bin al-Khattab (may Allah be pleased with him), who said: I heard the Messenger of Allah (peace be upon him), say:

"Actions are according to intentions, and everyone will get what was intended. Whoever migrates with an intention for Allah and His messenger, the migration will be for the sake of Allah and his Messenger. And whoever migrates for worldly gain or to marry a woman, then his migration will be for the sake of whatever he migrated for."

[Related by Bukhari & Muslim]

II. The Second Translation

`Umar, may Allaah be pleased with him, reported that the Messenger of Allaah, sallallaahu `alayhi wa sallam, said: "Actions are based on intentions, and everyone will have what they have intended. Whoever's migration was to Allaah and His Messenger, then their migration is to Allaah and His Messenger, but whoever's migration was for some parts of worldly life that they wished to acquire, or for a woman to marry, then their migration was for whatever they migrated for."

(Narrated by al-Bukhāri and Muslim)

III. The Third Translation

On the authority of the Commander of the Faithful, Abū Ḥafs, `Umar bin al-Khaṭṭāb, who said: I heard the Messenger of Allah (ﷺ) (peace be upon him), say:

"Deeds are only by intentions, and every man shall have only what he intended. So, one whose hijrah [emigration] was to Allah and His Messenger – his hijrah was to Allah and His Messenger. But one whose hijrah was to achieve a worldly aim or to a woman he would marry – then his hijrah was to that for which he emigrated."

(Narrated by al-Bukhāri and Muslim)

عَنْ عُمَرَ رَضِيَ اللهُ عَنْهُ أَيْضًا قَالَ:

" بَيْنَمَا نَحْنُ جُلُوسٌ عِنْدَ رَسُولِ اللهِ صلى الله عليه وسلم ذَاتَ يَوْمٍ، إِذْ طَلَعَ عَلَيْنَا رَجُلٌ شَدِيدُ بَيَاضِ الثِّيَابِ، شَدِيدُ سَوَادِ الشَّعْرِ، لَا يُرَى عَلَيْهِ أَثَرُ السَّفَرِ، وَلَا يَعْرِفُهُ مِنَّا أَحَدٌ. حَتَّى جَلَسَ إِلَى النَّبِيِّ صلى الله عليه وسلم. فَأَسْنَدَ رُكْبَتَيْهِ إِلَى رُكْبَتَيْهِ، وَوَضَعَ كَفَّيْهِ عَلَى فَخِذَيْهِ،

وَقَالَ: يَا مُحَمَّدُ أَخْبِرْنِي عَنِ الْإِسْلَامِ.

فَقَالَ رَسُولُ اللهِ صلى الله عليه وسلم الْإِسْلَامُ أَنْ تَشْهَدَ أَنْ لَا إِلَهَ إِلَّا اللهُ وَأَنَّ مُحَمَّدًا رَسُولُ اللهِ، وَتُقِيمَ الصَّلَاةَ، وَتُؤْتِيَ الزَّكَاةَ، وَتَصُومَ رَمَضَانَ، وَتَحُجَّ الْبَيْتَ إِنِ اسْتَطَعْتَ إِلَيْهِ سَبِيلًا.

قَالَ: صَدَقْتَ. فَعَجِبْنَا لَهُ يَسْأَلُهُ وَيُصَدِّقُهُ!

قَالَ: فَأَخْبِرْنِي عَنِ الْإِيمَانِ.

قَالَ: أَنْ تُؤْمِنَ بِاللهِ وَمَلَائِكَتِهِ وَكُتُبِهِ وَرُسُلِهِ وَالْيَوْمِ الْآخِرِ، وَتُؤْمِنَ بِالْقَدَرِ خَيْرِهِ وَشَرِّهِ.

قَالَ: صَدَقْتَ. قَالَ: فَأَخْبِرْنِي عَنِ الْإِحْسَانِ.

قَالَ: أَنْ تَعْبُدَ اللهَ كَأَنَّكَ تَرَاهُ، فَإِنْ لَمْ تَكُنْ تَرَاهُ فَإِنَّهُ يَرَاكَ.

قَالَ: فَأَخْبِرْنِي عَنِ السَّاعَةِ. قَالَ: مَا الْمَسْئُولُ عَنْهَا بِأَعْلَمَ مِنَ السَّائِلِ.

قَالَ: فَأَخْبِرْنِي عَنْ أَمَارَاتِهَا؟ قَالَ: أَنْ تَلِدَ الْأَمَةُ رَبَّتَهَا، وَأَنْ تَرَى الْحُفَاةَ الْعُرَاةَ الْعَالَةَ رِعَاءَ الشَّاءِ يَتَطَاوَلُونَ فِي الْبُنْيَانِ. ثُمّ انْطَلَقَ، فَلَبِثْتُ مَلِيًّا،

ثُمّ قَالَ: يَا عُمَرُ أَتَدْرِي مَنْ السَّائِلُ.

قُلْتُ: اللهُ وَرَسُولُهُ أَعْلَمُ.

قَالَ: فَإِنَّهُ جِبْرِيلُ أَتَاكُمْ يُعَلِّمُكُمْ دِينَكُمْ ".

[رَوَاهُ مُسْلِمٌ]

I. The First Translation

It was narrated on the authority of Umar (may Allah be pleased with him), who said:

While we were one day sitting with the Messenger of Allah (peace be upon him), there appeared before us a man dressed in extremely white clothes and with very black hair. No traces of journeying were visible on him, and none of us knew him. He sat down close by the Prophet (peace be upon him), rested his knee against his thighs, and said, "O Muhammad! Inform me about Islam."

The Messenger of Allah (peace be upon him) said, "Islam is that you should testify that there is no deity except Allah and that Muhammad is His Messenger, that you should perform salah, pay the Zakah, fast during Ramadan, and perform Hajj to the House, if you are able to do so."

The man said, "You have spoken truly." We were astonished at his questioning him (the Messenger) and telling him that he was right, but he went on to say, "Inform me about iman." He (the Messenger of Allah) answered, "It is that you believe in Allah and His angels and His Books and His Messengers and in the Last Day, and in qadar (fate), both in its good and in its evil aspects." He said, "You have spoken truly."

Then he (the man) said, "Inform me about Ihsan." He (the Messenger of Allah) answered, "It is that you should serve Allah as though you could see Him, for though you cannot see Him yet (know that) He sees you."

He said, "Inform me about the Hour." He (the Messenger of Allah) said, "About that, the one questioned knows no more than the questioner." So he said, "Well, inform me about the signs thereof." He said, "They are that the slave-girl will give birth to her mistress, that you will see the barefooted, naked, destitute, the herdsmen of the sheep (competing with each other) in raising lofty buildings." Thereupon the man went of. I waited a while, and then he (the Messenger of Allah) said, "O Umar, do you know who that questioner was?" I replied, "Allah and His Messenger know better." He said, "That was Jibril (the Angel Gabriel). He came to teach you your religion."

[Muslim]

II. The Second Translation

My father, `Umar ibn Al-Khattaab, may Allaah be pleased with him, informed me, saying: 'While we were sitting with Allaah's Messenger, sallallaahu `alayhi wa sallam, one day, a man who had an extremely white garment on, who had extremely black hair, and who did not have any traces of travel, came to us. None of us knew him. He sat with the Prophet, sallallaahu `alayhi wa sallam, so close that their knees touched. He placed his hands on his thighs and said: "O Muhammad, tell me about Islaam."

Allaah's Messenger, sallallaahu `alayhi wa sallam, said: "Islaam is to testify that there is no deity worthy of worship besides Allaah and that Muhammad is the Messenger of Allaah, establish prayer, give obligatory charity, fast Ramadhaan, and perform pilgrimage if you are able."

The man said: "You have stated the truth. "

We were amazed by him; he asked him, but then declared him as having told the truth.

Then, he said: "Tell me about faith."

Allaah's Messenger, sallallaahu `alayhi wa sallam, said: "It is to believe in Allaah, His angels, Books, messengers, the Last Day, and the good and bad parts of predestination."

The man said: "You have stated the truth. Tell me about

Ihsaan (perfection)."

The Prophet, sallallaahu `alayhi wa sallam, said: "It is to worship Allaah as if you see Him. If you cannot see Him, He Sees you."

The man said: "Tell me about the Hour."

The Prophet, sallallaahu `alayhi wa sallam, said: "The one being asked is no more knowledgeable than the one asking."

The man said: "Tell me of its signs."

The Prophet, sallallaahu `alayhi wa sallam, said: "It is when a slave girl gives birth to her master, and when you find barefoot, naked, poor shepherds competing in building structures."

Then, he left, and I remained for a short while. Then, Allaah's Messenger, sallallaahu `alayhi wa sallam, said: "O `Umar, do you know who that questioner was?"

I said: "Allaah and His Messenger know more."

He, sallallaahu `alayhi wa sallam, said: "That was Jibreel, may Allaah exalt his mention, who came to teach you your religion."

[Narrated by Muslim]

III. The Third Translation

Also on the authority of `Umar, who said: [One day] while we were sitting with the Messenger of Allah (🕌), a man came over to us whose clothes were exceedingly white and whose hair was exceedingly black; no signs of travel were seen on him, but none of us knew him. He came and sat down opposite the Prophet (ﷺ) and rested his knees against his, placing the palms of his hands on his thighs.

He said, "O Muḥammad, inform me about Islam."

The Messenger of Allah (ﷺ) said, "Islam is to testify that there is no god but Allah and that Muḥammad is the Messenger of Allah, to establish prayer, to give zakāh, to fast Ramadhān, and to make the pilgrimage to the House if you are able to do so."

He said, "You have spoken the truth,"

And we wondered at his asking him and confirming it.

He said, "Then inform me about īmān."

He said (ﷺ), "It is to believe in Allah, His angels, His books, His messengers, and the Last Day, and to believe in predestination, both the good and the evil thereof."

He said, "You have spoken the truth." He said, "Then inform me about iḥsān."

He said (ﷺ), "It is to worship Allah as though you see Him; if you do not see Him, indeed, He sees you."

He said, "Then inform me about the Hour."

He said (ﷺ), "The one questioned about it knows no more

than the questioner."

He said, "Then inform me of its signs."

He said (ﷺ), "That the slave-woman will give birth to her mistress and that you will see barefooted, naked, destitute shepherds competing in the loftiness of constructions."

Then he departed, and I stayed for a time. Then he said, "O ʿUmar, do you know who the questioner was?"

I said, "Allah and His Messenger are more knowing."

He said (ﷺ), "It was Gabriel. He came to you to teach you your religion."

[Narrated by Muslim]

Hadeeth: 3 الحديث:

عَنْ أَبِي عَبْدِ الرَّحْمَنِ عَبْدِ اللّهِ بْنِ عُمَرَ بْنِ الْخَطَّابِ رَضِيَ اللّهُ عَنْهُمَا قَالَ:
سَمِعْت رَسُولَ اللّهِ صلى الله عليه وسلم يَقُولُ:

"بُنِيَ الْإِسْلَامُ عَلَى خَمْسٍ: شَهَادَةِ أَنْ لَا إِلَهَ إِلَّا اللّهُ وَأَنَّ مُحَمَّدًا رَسُولُ اللّهِ، وَإِقَامِ
الصَّلَاةِ، وَإِيتَاءِ الزَّكَاةِ، وَحَجِّ الْبَيْتِ، وَصَوْمِ رَمَضَانَ".

رَوَاهُ: [الْبُخَارِيُّ] وَ [مُسْلِمٌ].

I.   The First Translation

On the authority of Abdullah ibn Umar ibn Al-Khattab (may
Allah be pleased with him) who said: I heard the Messenger
of Allah (peace be upon him) say:

Islam has been built on five [pillars]: testifying that there is no
god but Allah and that Muhammad is the Messenger of Allah,
performing the prayers, paying the Zakah, making the
pilgrimage to the House, and fasting in Ramadan.

[Related by Bukhari & Muslim]

II. The Second Translation

Ibn `Umar, may Allaah be pleased with him, reported that
Allaah's Messenger, sallallaahu `alayhi wa sallam, said:

"Islaam has been built on five: Testifying that there is no deity worthy of worship and that Muhammad is the Messenger of Allaah, establishing prayer, giving obligatory charity, pilgrimage, and fasting Ramadhaan."

[Narrated by al-Bukhāri and Muslim]

III. The Third Translation

On the authority of Abū ʿAbdur-Raḥmān, ʿAbdullāh, son of ʿUmar bin al-Khaṭṭāb, who said: I heard the Messenger of Allah (ﷺ) say:

"Islam has been built on five: testifying that there is no deity but Allah and that Muḥammad is the Messenger of Allah, the establishment of prayer, giving zakāh, making the pilgrimage to the House, and fasting Ramadhān."

[Narrated by al-Bukhāri and Muslim]

عَنْ أَبِي عَبْدِ الرَّحْمَنِ عَبْدِ اللّهِ بْنِ مَسْعُودٍ رَضِيَ اللّهُ عَنْهُ قَالَ:

حَدَّثَنَا رَسُولُ اللّهِ صلى الله عليه وسلم -وَهُوَ الصَّادِقُ الْمَصْدُوقُ-: "إِنَّ أَحَدَكُمْ يُجْمَعُ خَلْقُهُ فِي بَطْنِ أُمِّهِ أَرْبَعِينَ يَوْمًا نُطْفَةً، ثُمَّ يَكُونُ عَلَقَةً مِثْلَ ذَلِكَ، ثُمَّ يَكُونُ مُضْغَةً مِثْلَ ذَلِكَ، ثُمَّ يُرْسَلُ إِلَيْهِ الْمَلَكُ فَيَنْفُخُ فِيهِ الرُّوحَ، وَيُؤْمَرُ بِأَرْبَعِ كَلِمَاتٍ: بِكَتْبِ رِزْقِهِ، وَأَجَلِهِ، وَعَمَلِهِ، وَشَقِيٍّ أَمْ سَعِيدٍ؛ فَوَاللّهِ الَّذِي لَا إِلَهَ غَيْرُهُ إِنَّ أَحَدَكُمْ لَيَعْمَلُ بِعَمَلِ أَهْلِ الْجَنَّةِ حَتَّى مَا يَكُونُ بَيْنَهُ وَبَيْنَهَا إِلَّا ذِرَاعٌ فَيَسْبِقُ عَلَيْهِ الْكِتَابُ فَيَعْمَلُ بِعَمَلِ أَهْلِ النَّارِ فَيَدْخُلُهَا. وَإِنَّ أَحَدَكُمْ لَيَعْمَلُ بِعَمَلِ أَهْلِ النَّارِ حَتَّى مَا يَكُونُ بَيْنَهُ وَبَيْنَهَا إِلَّا ذِرَاعٌ فَيَسْبِقُ عَلَيْهِ الْكِتَابُ فَيَعْمَلُ بِعَمَلِ أَهْلِ الْجَنَّةِ فَيَدْخُلُهَا".

رَوَاهُ: [الْبُخَارِيُّ] وَ [مُسْلِمٌ].

I.   The First Translation

On the authority of Abdullah ibn Masud (may Allah be pleased with him), who said: The Messenger of Allah (peace be upon him), and he is the truthful and the believed, narrated to us:

Verily the creation of each one of you is brought together in his mother's womb for forty days in the form of a drop, then he becomes a clot of blood for a like period, then a morsel of flesh for a like period, then there is sent to him the angel who blows the breath of life into him and who is commanded with four matters: to write down his sustenance, his life span, his actions, and whether he will be happy or unhappy (whether or not he will enter Paradise).

By Allah, other than Whom there is no deity, verily one of you performs the actions of the people of Paradise until there is but an arm's length between him and it, and that which has been written overtakes him, and so he acts with the actions of the people of the Hellfire and thus enters it; and verily one of you performs the actions of the people of the Hellfire, until there is but an arm's length between him and it, and that which has been written overtakes him and so he acts with the actions of the people of Paradise and thus he enters it.

[Related by Bukhari & Muslim]

II. The Second Translation

`Abdullaah ibn Mas`ood, may Allaah be pleased with him, said: The Messenger of Allaah, the truthful and believed one, sallallaahu `alayhi wa sallam, said:

'The creation of each one of you is brought together in their mother's womb for forty days in the form of a drop, then they become a clot of blood for a similar period, then a morsel of flesh for a similar period, then there is sent to him the angel who blows his soul into him and who is commanded with four matters: the angel is ordered to write their sustenance, lifespan, their actions, and if they will be happy or miserable. By the One besides Whom there is no deity worthy of worship, one of you would do the actions of the people of Paradise until there is merely a hand span between them and Paradise, but what was predestined overtakes them, causing them to do actions of the people of Hellfire, and they enter Hellfire. Also, one of you would do the actions of the people of Hellfire until they are merely a hand span away from Hellfire, but what was predestined overtakes them, causing them to do actions of the people of Paradise, and they enter Paradise.'"

[Narrated by al-Bukhāri and Muslim]

عَنْ أُمِّ الْمُؤْمِنِينَ أُمِّ عَبْدِ اللهِ عَائِشَةَ رَضِيَ اللّهُ عَنْهَا، قَالَتْ: قَالَ: رَسُولُ اللّهِ

صلى الله عليه وسلم:

"مَنْ أَحْدَثَ فِي أَمْرِنَا هَذَا مَا لَيْسَ مِنْهُ فَهُوَ رَدٌّ."

رَوَاهُ: [الْبُخَارِيُّ] وَ [مُسْلِمٌ].

وَفِي رِوَايَةٍ لِمُسْلِمٍ:

"مَنْ عَمِلَ عَمَلًا لَيْسَ عَلَيْهِ أَمْرُنَا فَهُوَ رَدٌّ".

I. The First Translation

On the authority of the mother of the faithful, 'Aisha (may Allah be pleased with her), who said: The Messenger of Allah (peace be upon him) said:

He who innovates something in this matter of ours [Islam] that is not of it will have it rejected [by Allah].

[Bukhari & Muslim]

In one version by [Muslim] it reads:

He who does an act which we have not commanded, will have it rejected [by Allah].

II. The Second Translation

`Aa'ishah, may Allaah be pleased with her, reported that the Messenger of Allaah, sallallaahu `alayhi wa sallam, said: "Whoever invents something in this affair of ours that is not a part of it will have it rejected."

[Narrated by al-Bukhāri and Muslim]

III. The Third Translation

On the authority of the Mother of the Believers, Umm `Abdullāh, `Ā'ishah, who said: The Messenger of Allah (ﷺ) said:

"He who innovates something in this matter of ours that is not a part of it – it will be rejected."

[Narrated by al-Bukhāri and Muslim]

In one version by [Muslim] it says:

"He who does a deed not in accordance with our matter – it will be rejected."

Hadeeth: 6 الحديث:

عَنْ أَبِي عَبْدِ اللَّهِ النُّعْمَانِ بْنِ بَشِيرٍ رَضِيَ اللَّهُ عَنْهُمَا، قَالَ: سَمِعْتُ رَسُولَ اللَّهِ صلى الله عليه وسلم يَقُولُ:

"إِنَّ الْحَلَالَ بَيِّنٌ، وَإِنَّ الْحَرَامَ بَيِّنٌ، وَبَيْنَهُمَا أُمُورٌ مُشْتَبِهَاتٌ لَا يَعْلَمُهُنَّ كَثِيرٌ مِنَ النَّاسِ، فَمَنِ اتَّقَى الشُّبُهَاتِ فَقَدِ اسْتَبْرَأَ لِدِينِهِ وَعِرْضِهِ، وَمَنْ وَقَعَ فِي الشُّبُهَاتِ وَقَعَ فِي الْحَرَامِ، كَالرَّاعِي يَرْعَى حَوْلَ الْحِمَى يُوشِكُ أَنْ يَرْتَعَ فِيهِ، أَلَا وَإِنَّ لِكُلِّ مَلِكٍ حِمًى، أَلَا وَإِنَّ حِمَى اللَّهِ مَحَارِمُهُ، أَلَا وَإِنَّ فِي الْجَسَدِ مُضْغَةً إِذَا صَلَحَتْ صَلَحَ الْجَسَدُ كُلُّهُ، وَإِذَا فَسَدَتْ فَسَدَ الْجَسَدُ كُلُّهُ، أَلَا وَهِيَ الْقَلْبُ".

رَوَاهُ: [الْبُخَارِيُّ] وَ [مُسْلِمٌ].

I. The First Translation

On the authority of Abu 'Abdullah al-Nu'man bin Bashir (may Allah be pleased with him) who said: I heard the Messenger of Allah (sallallaahu `alayhi wa sallam) say:

"The halal is clear and the haram is clear, and between them are matters unclear that are unknown to most people. Whoever is wary of these unclear matters has absolved his religion and honor. And whoever indulges in them has indulged in the haram. It is like a shepherd who herds his sheep too close to preserved sanctuary, and they will eventually graze in it. Every king has a sanctuary, and the sanctuary of Allah is what He has made haram. There lies within the body a piece of flesh. If it is sound, the whole body is sound; and if it is corrupted, the whole body is corrupted. Verily this piece is the heart."

[Bukhari & Muslim]

II. The Second Translation

An-Nu`maan ibn Basheer, may Allaah be pleased with him, reported that the Messenger of Allaah, sallallaahu `alayhi wa sallam, said:

"The lawful is clear, and the unlawful is clear, and there are matters between them that are unclear that not many people know of. Whoever avoids the unclear matters saves their religion and honor from being blamed, but whoever falls into the unclear matters has fallen into unlawful matters. It is similar to a shepherd herding their sheep close to a restricted land; they will imminently fall into it. Every king has a restricted area, and the restricted area of Allaah is His prohibitions. In the heart, there is a piece of flesh, if it is upright, the rest of the body follows, and if it is corrupted, the rest of the body follows. The piece of flesh is the heart."

[Narrated by al-Bukhāri and Muslim]

III. The Third Translation

On the authority of Abū ʿAbdullāh, an-Nuʿmān bin Basheer, who said: I heard the Messenger of Allah (ﷺ) say:

"The lawful is clear, and the unlawful is clear, and between the two of them are doubtful matters about which many people do not know. So he who avoids doubtful matters has sought to clear himself in regard to his religion and his honor, but he who falls into doubtful matters [then] falls into the unlawful, like the shepherd who pastures around a private area, all but grazing therein. Undoubtedly, every sovereign has private property, and indeed, the private property of Allah is His prohibited matters. Undoubtedly, within the body is a morsel of flesh which, when it is good, the whole body is good; but when it is corrupt, the whole body is corrupt. Indeed, it is the heart."

[Narrated by al-Bukhāri and Muslim]

عَنْ أَبِي رُقَيَّةَ تَمِيمٍ بْنِ أَوْسٍ الدَّارِيِّ رَضِيَ اللهُ عَنْهُ أَنَّ النَّبِيَّ صلى الله عليه وسلم قَالَ:

"الدِّينُ النَّصِيحَةُ." قُلْنَا: لِمَنْ؟ قَالَ: "لِلّهِ، وَلِكِتَابِهِ، وَلِرَسُولِهِ، وَلِأَئِمَّةِ الْمُسْلِمِينَ، وَعَامَّتِهِمْ."

[رَوَاهُ مُسْلِمٌ]

I.   The First Translation

On the authority of Tamim Al-Dari (may Allah be pleased with him):

The Prophet (peace be upon him) said, "The religion is naseehah (sincerity)." We said, "To whom?" He (peace be upon him) said, "To Allah, His Book, His Messenger, and to the leaders of the Muslims and their common folk."

[Muslim]

II. The Second Translation

On the authority of Abū Ruqayyah, Tameem bin Aus ad-Dāri, that the Prophet (ﷺ) said: "Religion is sincerity." We said, "To whom?" He said, "To Allah and to His Book, to His Messenger, and to the leaders of Muslims and their common people."

[Narrated by Muslim]

Hadeeth: 8 الحديث:

عَنْ ابْنِ عُمَرَ رَضِيَ اللّهُ عَنْهُمَا، أَنَّ رَسُولَ اللّهِ صلى الله عليه وسلم قَالَ:

"أُمِرْتُ أَنْ أُقَاتِلَ النَّاسَ حَتَّى يَشْهَدُوا أَنْ لَا إِلَهَ إِلَّا اللّهُ وَأَنَّ مُحَمَّدًا رَسُولُ اللّهِ،

وَيُقِيمُوا الصَّلَاةَ، وَيُؤْتُوا الزَّكَاةَ؛ فَإِذَا فَعَلُوا ذَلِكَ عَصَمُوا مِنِّي دِمَاءَهُمْ

وَأَمْوَالَهُمْ إِلَّا بِحَقِّ الْإِسْلَامِ، وَحِسَابُهُمْ عَلَى اللّهِ تَعَالَى".

رَوَاهُ: [الْبُخَارِيُّ] وَ [مُسْلِمٌ].

I.   The First Translation

On the authority of Abdullah ibn Umar (may Allah be pleased with him), the Messenger of Allah (peace be upon him) said:

I have been ordered to fight against the people until they testify that there is none worthy of worship except Allah and that Muhammad is the Messenger of Allah, and until they establish the Salah and pay the Zakah. And if they do so then they will have gained protection from me for their lives and property, unless [they commit acts that are punishable] in accordance to Islam, and their reckoning will be with Allah the Almighty.

[Al-Bukhari & Muslim]

Commentary

Different Narrations

This hadith has many different narrations. Some of them actually say that "I was commanded to fight the people" and then the narrators would add in right there "meaning the polytheist" or some would say "I was commanded to fight the people until they bear witness that there is no God but Allah, and that Muhammad is His messenger." There is no mention of prayer and fasting, and there are various different narrations within these lines.

One important thing to take into account is that whenever the Prophet Muhammad says, "I was commanded" in this passive form, then that means that the demand is coming directly from Allah.

Who Are "The People"?

So, what does it mean when he says, "to fight the people"? This is the most controversial and misunderstood part of the hadith. Does "people" refer to everyone, a certain group, or is there further context to this hadith? Based on the context of the life of the Prophet (sallallaahu `alayhi wa sallam), and the actions of the generations after him, it's understood that this hadith does not refer to all people, by any means. There were many people that he didn't fight and people with whom we had peace contracts. There were also people that paid jizya. They were not Muslims, but they paid this tax to the Muslim state in order to be protected and to receive services.

Ibn Hajar Al-Asqalani (may Allah be pleased with him), in his explanation of Sahih Al Bukhari, mentions five or six different possibilities for what "the people" could mean. The main point in that discussion is that the hadith refers to a particular type of people.

One specific incident that occurred, related to the context of this hadith, is that a group of people decided that they would no longer pay zakah when Abu Bakr became the leader of the Muslim nation. Abu Bakr took the stance that he would fight them unless they paid zakah. Many of the other companions disagreed with him, and Abu Bakr would refer to this narration, and others would refer to the narrations that don't have the mention of establishing prayer and paying zakah.

Umar (may Allah be pleased with him) disagreed with him and argued with him for a while. Umar later said, "When I saw that Allah had made Abu Bakr so convinced with his opinion, then I, myself, also become convinced with his opinion." Abu Bakr said that you couldn't distinguish between these things. They are all fundamentals of the faith and cannot be denied, in particular establishing prayer and paying zakah because of this narration.

The Right of Islam

Another point to mention is that when the believers start to establish prayer and pay zakah, they gain protection from Allah (swt) for their lives and property, unless they commit acts that are punishable in Islam, such as murder or adultery. It is important to remember that this whole discussion revolved around the responsibilities of a Muslim state, and does not really apply to us. However, what does apply to us, directly, is the issue of whether this statement means that Muslims are commanded to fight all mankind. The answer is no, based on what was said before and specifically looking at the life of the Prophet (sallallaahu `alayhi wa sallam).

"Struggle"

There is an ongoing discussion about the meaning of jihad in Islam. Jihad is not holy war. It means struggle, and it is a very important concept in Islam. It can refer to the struggle of an individual against oneself, speaking the word of truth in front of a tyrant, actual physical defense, or a battle that occurs on the battlefield. It's a central concept in Islam, but it needs to be understood correctly and in a balanced and truthful way.

II. The Second Translation

Ibn `Umar, may Allaah be pleased with him, reported that the Messenger of Allaah, sallallaahu `alayhi wa sallam, said:

"I have been ordered to fight the people until they testify that there is no deity worthy of worship besides Allaah and that Muhammad is the Messenger of Allaah, establish prayer, and give obligatory charity. If they do so, then their wealth and blood are protected from me except through the right of Islaam, and their accounting is with Allaah the Exalted."

[Narrated by al-Bukhāri and Muslim]

III. The Third Translation

On the authority of 'Abdullāh, the son of 'Umar bin al-Khaṭṭāb that the Messenger of Allah (ﷺ) said:

"I have been ordered to fight people until they testify that there is no god but Allah and that Muḥammad is the Messenger of Allah and perform the prayers and give the zakāh. If they do that, they are protected from me regarding their blood and their properties unless by the right of Islam, and their account will be with Allah, the Exalted."

[Narrated by al-Bukhāri and Muslim]

Commentary

Jihād is one of the most important religious duties in Islam and remains so until the Day of Judgement. It is declared by the head of an Islamic state and supported by the community as a whole. It is not aimed at forcing belief on any people, for the Qur'ān states:

$$\lll \lambda \ \text{إِكْرَاهَ فِى ٱلدِّينِ} \ggg$$

(سورة البقرة، **256**)

{There shall be no compulsion in religion}

(Sūrah al-Baqarah, 256)

In the acceptance of religion. Rather, its purpose is the removal of obstacles to the propagation of Islam and to free thought and choice in the matter, and then the establishment of a force sufficient to uphold this freedom, insure justice and protect Muslims from persecution and oppression. When the Prophet (ﷺ) was commanded by Allah to fight following the hijrah(emigration to al-Madinah) and establishment of the state, Muslims were being persecuted within the Arabian peninsula by the Quraysh and outside its borders by the Persian and Byzantine establishments. Thus, he (ﷺ) was to first liberate the Muslims by subduing opposition among the Arabs, then to continue jihād wherever Islam was opposed until men could worship Allah freely and invite others to Islam. The "people" to be fought are those who either attack or persecute Muslims and those who strive to prevent the natural spread of Islam through peaceful means, i.e., through da'wah(invitation) and teaching. They may also include apostates, although this category is usually considered separately under "the right of Islam." It is known that the Messenger of Allah (ﷺ) accepted as a Muslim anyone who pronounced the shahādah and regarded his declaration of faith adequate to protect him from being harmed. He required no immediate proof of the person's sincerity and thus strongly rebuked Usāmah bin Zayd for killing a man whom he assumed had said "Lā illāh ill-Allāh" only to save himself. Once a person enters Islam, however, he is expected to fulfill its obligations. A Muslim may be fought by the state for refusing to pray or to give zakāh (unlike fasting and ḥajj), this having been understood by the ṣaḥābah as a part of the "right of Islam." Hence, with the concurrence of other eminent ṣaḥābah, Abū Bakr fought the withholders of zakāh after the death of the Prophet (ﷺ) until they finally relented, while some of them, who refused, left the religion altogether. Prayer and zakāh are mentioned specifically in the Qur'ān as proof of Islam and protection for those who observe them:

﴿ فَإِن تَابُواْ وَأَقَامُواْ ٱلصَّلَوٰةَ وَءَاتَوُاْ ٱلزَّكَوٰةَ فَخَلُّواْ سَبِيلَهُمْ ﴾

(سورة التوبة، **5**)

{But if they repent, establish prayer and give zakāh, let them go on their way}

(Sūrah at-Tawbah, 5)

﴿ فَإِن تَابُواْ وَأَقَامُواْ ٱلصَّلَوٰةَ وَءَاتَوُاْ ٱلزَّكَوٰةَ فَإِخْوَٰنُكُمْ فِى ٱلدِّينِ ﴾

(سورة التوبة، **11**)

{But if they repent, establish prayer and give zakāh, they are your brothers in religion}

(Sūrah at-Tawbah, 11)

These verses show that refusal of those two obligations is the reason for continued war against them by the Islamic state. The "right of Islam" also encompasses the death penalty carried out for capital offenses – those mentioned in the sunnah, i.e., murder, adultery and apostasy,49 or in the Qur'ān, i.e., ḥirābah, which includes acts of violence and terrorism against individuals and those of treason and aggression against the Muslim leadership. Mention of the account with Allah confirms that not every Muslim is sincere in what he professes or does. Hypocrites took care to be seen praying in the mosques in order to insure their safety, and the Prophet (ﷺ) did not permit the killing of anyone who appeared outwardly to be a Muslim in spite of his own knowledge about them. Scholars have agreed that declaration of Islam followed by the outward evidence of prayer and zakāh gives one all the rights of a Muslim, including that of protection. If one does that for a worldly benefit, out of fear of death, or dishonestly, such as one who prays without ablution or eats while claiming to be fasting, then Allah is most knowing of him and will judge his deeds accordingly in the Hereafter. But if he is sincere in faith and intention, performing these and other obligations to the best of his ability out of consciousness of Allah, then he is among the ranks of the believers and can expect his full reward.

عَنْ أَبِي هُرَيْرَةَ عَبْدِ الرَّحْمَنِ بْنِ صَخْرٍ رَضِيَ اللّهُ عَنْهُ قَالَ: سَمِعْت رَسُولَ اللّهِ
صلى الله عليه وسلم يَقُولُ:

"مَا نَهَيْتُكُمْ عَنْهُ فَاجْتَنِبُوهُ، وَمَا أَمَرْتُكُمْ بِهِ فَأْتُوا مِنْهُ مَا اسْتَطَعْتُمْ، فَإِنَّمَا
أَهْلَكَ الَّذِينَ مِنْ قَبْلِكُمْ كَثْرَةُ مَسَائِلِهِمْ وَاخْتِلَافُهُمْ عَلَى أَنْبِيَائِهِمْ ".

رَوَاهُ: [الْبُخَارِيُّ] وَ [مُسْلِمٌ].

I.   The First Translation

On the authority of Abu Hurayrah (may Allah be pleased with him) who said: I heard the Messenger of Allah (peace be upon him) say:

What I have forbidden for you, avoid. What I have ordered you [to do], do as much of it as you can. For verily, it was only their excessive questioning and disagreeing with their Prophets that destroyed [the nations] who were before you.

[Bukhari & Muslim]

II. The Second Translation

Abu Hurayrah, may Allaah be pleased with him, reported that he heard Allaah's Messenger, sallallaahu `alayhi wa sallam, say:

"Anything I prohibit you from doing, then abstain from it, and anything I order you to do, then do as much of it as you are able. Those who have come before you were destroyed because of their constant questioning and bickering with their prophets."

[Narrated by al-Bukhāri and Muslim

عَنْ أَبِي هُرَيْرَةَ رَضِيَ اللهُ عَنْهُ قَالَ:

قَالَ رَسُولُ اللهِ صلى الله عليه وسلم "إِنَّ اللهَ طَيِّبٌ لَا يَقْبَلُ إِلَّا طَيِّبًا، وَإِنَّ اللهَ أَمَرَ الْمُؤْمِنِينَ بِمَا أَمَرَ بِهِ الْمُرْسَلِينَ،

فَقَالَ تَعَالَى: ﴿ يَا أَيُّهَا الرُّسُلُ كُلُوا مِنْ الطَّيِّبَاتِ وَاعْمَلُوا صَالِحًا ﴾

وَقَالَ تَعَالَى: ﴿ يَا أَيُّهَا الَّذِينَ آمَنُوا كُلُوا مِنْ طَيِّبَاتِ مَا رَزَقْنَاكُمْ ﴾

ثُمَّ ذَكَرَ الرَّجُلَ يُطِيلُ السَّفَرَ أَشْعَثَ أَغْبَرَ يَمُدُّ يَدَيْهِ إِلَى السَّمَاءِ: يَا رَبِّ! يَا رَبِّ! وَمَطْعَمُهُ حَرَامٌ، وَمَشْرَبُهُ حَرَامٌ، وَمَلْبَسُهُ حَرَامٌ، وَغُذِّيَ بِالْحَرَامِ، فَأَنَّى يُسْتَجَابُ لَهُ؟".

رَوَاهُ: [الْبُخَارِيُّ] وَ [مُسْلِمٌ].

I.   The First Translation

On the authority of Abu Hurayrah (may Allah be pleased with him) who said: The Messenger of Allah (peace be upon him) said:

"Allah the Almighty is good and accepts only that which is good. And verily Allah has commanded the believers to do that which He has commanded the Messengers. So, the Almighty has said:

{O (you) Messengers! Eat of the tayyibat (good things), and perform righteous deeds}

[Sūrah al-Mu'minūn, 51]

And the Almighty has said:

{O you who believe! Eat of the lawful things that We have provided you}

[Sūrah al-Baqarah, 172].

Then he (peace be upon him) mentioned a man who, having journeyed far, is dishevelled and dusty, and who spreads out his hands to the sky saying, "O Lord! O Lord!" while his food is haram, his drink is haram, his clothing is haram, and he has been nourished with haram, so how can [his supplication] be answered?"

[Bukhari & Muslim]

II. The Second Translation

Abu Hurayrah, may Allaah be pleased with him, narrated that Allaah's Messenger, sallallaahu `alayhi wa sallam, said: "O people! Allaah is Pure, and only accepts purity, and Allaah has ordered the believers with the same that He ordered the Messengers, Saying:

{O messengers, eat from the good foods and work righteousness. Indeed, I, of what you do, am Knowing.}

[QUR'AAN 23:51]

And:

{O you who have believed, eat from the good things which We have provided for you.}

[QUR'AAN 2:172]

Then, he mentioned the situation of a man who travels far away, is dirty and unkempt, but raises his hands to the sky, stating: 'O Lord, O Lord,' while his food, drink, clothes, and nourishment are all unlawful, so, how can his supplication be answered?

[Narrated by al-Bukhāri and Muslim]

III. The Third Translation

On the authority of Abū Hurayrah, who reported that the Messenger of Allah (ﷺ) said:

"Indeed, Allah, the Exalted, is pure and accepts only that which is pure. Allah has commanded the believers to do what he commanded the messengers, and He, the Exalted, said:

{O messengers, eat of the good things and work righteousness.}

[Sūrah al-Mu'minūn, 51]

And He, the Exalted, said:

{O you who have believed, eat from the good things with which We have provided you.}

[Sūrah al-Baqarah, 172].

Then he mentioned a man who has prolonged a journey, is disheveled and dusty and extends his hands to the heaven, [supplicating], 'Our Lord, Our Lord,' while his food is unlawful, his drink is unlawful, his clothing is unlawful, and he has been nourished by what is unlawful; so how could he be answered?"

[Narrated by al-Bukhāri and Muslim]

عَنْ أَبِي مُحَمَّدٍ الْحَسَنِ بْنِ عَلِيّ بْنِ أَبِي طَالِبٍ سِبْطِ رَسُولِ اللَّهِ صلى الله عليه

وسلم وَرَيْحَانَتِهِ رَضِيَ اللَّهُ عَنْهُمَا، قَالَ:

حَفِظْت مِنْ رَسُولِ اللَّهِ صلى الله عليه وسلم "دَعْ مَا يُرِيبُك إِلَى مَا لَا يُرِيبُك".

رَوَاهُ: [التِّرْمِذِيُّ] وَ [وَالنَّسَائِيُّ]، وَقَالَ التِّرْمِذِيُّ: حَدِيثٌ حَسَنٌ صَحِيحٌ.

I.   The First Translation

On the authority of Abu Muhammad al-Hasan ibn Ali ibn
Abee Talib (may Allah be pleased with him), the grandson of
the Messenger of Allah (peace and blessings of Allah be upon
him), and the one much loved by him, who said:

I memorized from the Messenger of Allah (peace and
blessings of Allah be upon him):

"Leave what makes you doubtful for what does not."

[Related by Tirmidhi & Nasai]

II. The Second Translation

Al-Hasan ibn `Ali, the grandson of Allaah's Messenger,
sallallaahu `alayhi wa sallam, and his beloved, said that he
memorized that Allaah's Messenger, sallallaahu `alayhi wa
sallam, said: "Leave what is doubtful to you in favor of what is
not doubtful to you."

**[Reported by An-Nasaa'i, and At-Tirmithi who ruled it as
Hasan Saheeh (acceptably authentic).]**

III. The Third Translation

On the authority of Abū Muḥammad, al-Ḥasan, son of ʿAli bin Abī Ṭālib and grandson of the Messenger of Allah (ﷺ) and his fragrant [i.e., beloved] one, who said:

I memorized from the Messenger of Allah (ﷺ): "Leave that which makes you doubt for that which does not make you doubt."

[Narrated by an-Nasāʾi and at-Tirmidhi, who graded it as ḥasan-ṣaheeḥ]

Hadeeth: 12 الحديث:

عَنْ أَبِي هُرَيْرَةَ رَضِيَ اللهُ عَنْهُ قَالَ: قَالَ رَسُولُ اللَّهِ صلى الله عليه وسلم
"مِنْ حُسْنِ إِسْلَامِ الْمَرْءِ تَرْكُهُ مَا لَا يَعْنِيهِ".

حَدِيثٌ حَسَنٌ، رَوَاهُ التِّرْمِذِيُّ [رقم: 2318]، ابن ماجه [رقم: 3976]

I. The First Translation

On the authority of Abu Hurayrah (may Allah be pleased with him) who said: The Messenger of Allah (peace be upon him) said:

"Part of the perfection of one's Islam is his leaving that which does not concern him."

[Related by Tirmidhi]

II. The Second Translation

Abu Hurayrah, may Allaah be pleased with him, reported that the Prophet, sallallaahu 'alayhi wa sallam, said:

"A part of a person's good Islaam is that they abandon what does not concern them."

[Reported by At-Tirmithi (2317) Ibn Maajah (3976) and Ahmad (1737). At-Tirmithi ruled it as acceptable]

III. The Third Translation

On the authority of Abū Hurayrah, who said: The Messenger of Allah () said:

"From the excellence of a person's Islam is his leaving alone what does not concern him."

[Narrated by at-Tirmidhi and others in this form – ḥadīth ḥasan]

Hadeeth: 13 الحديث:

عَنْ أَبِي حَمْزَةَ أَنَسِ بْنِ مَالِكٍ رَضِيَ اللهُ عَنْهُ خَادِمِ رَسُولِ اللّهِ صلى الله عليه وسلم عَنِ النَّبِيِّ صلى الله عليه وسلم قَالَ:

"لَا يُؤْمِنُ أَحَدُكُمْ حَتَّى يُحِبَّ لِأَخِيهِ مَا يُحِبُّ لِنَفْسِهِ".

رَوَاهُ: [الْبُخَارِيُّ] وَ [مُسْلِمٌ].

I. The First Translation

On the authority of Abu Hamzah Anas bin Malik (may Allah be pleased with him) - the servant of the Messenger of Allah (peace and blessings of Allah be upon him) - that the Prophet (peace and blessings of Allah be upon him) said :

"None of you will believe until you love for your brother what you love for yourself."

[Related by Bukhari & Muslim]

II. The Second Translation

Abu Hamzah Anas ibn Maalik, may Allaah be pleased with him, reported that the Prophet, sallallaahu `alayhi wa sallam, said:

"One of you does not believe until they love for their brother or sister what they love for themselves."

[Reported by Al-Bukhaari (13) and Muslim (45).]

III. The Third Translation

On the authority of Abū Ḥamzah, Anas bin Mālik, the servant of the Messenger of Allah (ﷺ), that the Prophet (ﷺ) said:

"None of you [truly] believes until he likes for his brother what he likes for himself."

[Narrated by al-Bukhāri and Muslim]

Hadeeth: 14 الحديث:

عَنْ ابْنِ مَسْعُودٍ رَضِيَ اللهُ عَنْهُ قَالَ: قَالَ رَسُولُ اللَّهِ صلى الله عليه وسلم:

"لَا يَحِلُّ دَمُ امْرِئٍ مُسْلِمٍ [يشهد أن لا إله إلا الله، وأني رسول الله] إلَّا بِإِحْدَى

ثَلَاثٍ: الثَّيِّبُ الزَّانِي، وَالنَّفْسُ بِالنَّفْسِ، وَالتَّارِكُ لِدِينِهِ الْمُفَارِقُ لِلْجَمَاعَةِ".

رَوَاهُ: [الْبُخَارِيُّ] وَ [مُسْلِمٌ].

I.   The First Translation

On the authority of Abdullah Ibn Masud (may Allah be pleased with him) who said: The Messenger of Allah (peace be upon him) said:

"It is not permissible to spill the blood of a Muslim except in three [instances]: the married person who commits adultery, a life for a life, and the one who forsakes his religion and separates from the community."

[Related by Bukhari & Muslim]

Commentary

Ruling Only for Government

Someone's blood and life is a very big issue. It is not something that you can take into your own hands; it's not something to be decided by mere opinion. It is something that must be established and known through textual sources. The text has to be there and it is what clarifies whether or not there is any opening or discussion to these issues. In addition, they are issues of capital punishment and governance. They are not issues of personal vendettas or grudges carried out by individuals. They have to be carried out by governmental bodies.

The Prophet (peace be upon him)) had many roles in the society, and amongst those roles he ran a state, he was a judge, and he gave opinions to people according to the religion. If it was something he did as a ruler or a judge, then we have to leave it that way, and it should not be something that applies to everyone else's personal behavior. The topic of this hadith is a topic of governance and so it does not really apply to Muslims in the West.

II. The Second Translation

`Abdullaah ibn Mas`ood, may Allaah be pleased with him, reported that Allaah's Messenger, sallallaahu `alayhi wa sallam, said:

"The blood of a Muslim who testifies that there is no deity worthy of worship besides Allaah and that I am the messenger of Allaah is only made lawful through one of three things: Adultery, retribution, and abandonment of one's religion and parting with the congregation."

[Reported by Al-Bukhaari (6878) and Muslim (1676).]

III. The Third Translation

On the authority of Ibn Mas'ūd, who said: The Messenger of Allah (ﷺ) said:

"The blood of a Muslim person is not permitted [to be shed] except in one of three [cases]: the married adulterer, a life for a life, and the renouncer of his religion, the deserter of the community."

[Narrated by al-Bukhāri and Muslim]

Commentary

He sanctity of a Muslim life is confirmed by the Prophet (ﷺ) in this ḥadīth. The three stated exceptions are those where legal execution is carried out by the state (Not independent groups or individuals) to protect society from the spread of corruption. It may be compared to the surgical removal of a hopelessly diseased limb or organ which, although painful, restores the rest of a body to health. The death penalty, like the lesser prescribed (ḥadd) punishments, may only be carried out after a conviction completely free of the least doubt. It must further be established that the accused had reached puberty, was in full mental capacity at the time of the crime, and did not act under any form of coercion.

عَنْ أَبِي هُرَيْرَةَ رَضِيَ اللهُ عَنْهُ أَنَّ رَسُولَ اللّهِ صلى الله عليه وسلم قَالَ:

"مَنْ كَانَ يُؤْمِنُ بِاللّهِ وَالْيَوْمِ الْآخِرِ فَلْيَقُلْ خَيْرًا أَوْ لِيَصْمُتْ، وَمَنْ كَانَ يُؤْمِنُ بِاللّهِ وَالْيَوْمِ الْآخِرِ فَلْيُكْرِمْ جَارَهُ، وَمَنْ كَانَ يُؤْمِنُ بِاللّهِ وَالْيَوْمِ الْآخِرِ فَلْيُكْرِمْ ضَيْفَهُ".

رَوَاهُ: [الْبُخَارِيُّ] وَ [مُسْلِمٌ].

I. The First Translation

On the authority of Abu Hurayrah (may Allah be pleased with him), that the Messenger of Allah (peace be upon him) said:

"Let him who believes in Allah and the Last Day speak good, or keep silent; and let him who believes in Allah and the Last Day be generous to his neighbour; and let him who believes in Allah and the Last Day be generous to his guest."

[Related by Bukhari & Muslim]

II. The Second Translation

Abu Hurayrah, may Allaah be pleased with him, reported that Allaah's Messenger, sallallaahu `alayhi wa sallam, said:

"Whoever believes in Allaah and the Last Day should either say something good, or remain silent. Whoever believes in Allaah and the Last Day should honor their neighbor.

Whoever believes in Allaah and the Last Day should honor their guest."

[Reported by Al-Bukhaari (6018) and Muslim (47).]

III. The Third Translation

On the authority of Abū Hurayrah that the Messenger of Allah (ﷺ) said:

"One who believes in Allah and the Last Day should either speak good or keep silent, and one who believes in Allah and the Last Day should be generous to his neighbor, and one who believes in Allah and the Last Day should be generous to his guest."

[Narrated by al-Bukhāri and Muslim]

Hadeeth: 16 الحديث:

عَنْ أَبِي هُرَيْرَةَ رَضِيَ اللهُ عَنْهُ أَنَّ رَجُلًا قَالَ لِلنَّبِيِّ صلى الله عليه وسلم أَوْصِنِي. قَالَ:

"لَا تَغْضَبْ، فَرَدَّدَ مِرَارًا، قَالَ: لَا تَغْضَبْ".

رَوَاهُ: [الْبُخَارِيُّ]

I. The First Translation

On the authority of Abu Hurayrah (may Allah be pleased with him):

"A man said to the Prophet, 'Give me advice.' The Prophet, peace be upon him, said, 'Do not get angry.' The man asked repeatedly and the Prophet answered each time, 'Do not get angry.'"

[Related by Bukhari]

II. The Second Translation

Abu Hurayrah, may Allaah be pleased with him, reported that someone said to the Prophet of Allaah, sallallaahu `alayhi wa sallam: "Give me advice."

The Prophet of Allaah, sallallaahu `alayhi wa sallam, said:

"Do not become angry."

The man repeated his question numerous times, and the

Prophet of Allaah, sallallaahu `alayhi wa sallam, kept saying: "Do not become angry."

[Reported by Al-Bukhaari (6116)]

III. The Third Translation

On the authority of Abū Hurayrah, who said: A man said to the Prophet (ﷺ): "Counsel me."

He (ﷺ) said, "Do not get angry."

The man repeated [his request] several times.

He (ﷺ) said, "Do not get angry."

[Narrated by al-Bukhāri]

عَنْ أَبِي يَعْلَى شَدَّادِ بْنِ أَوْسٍ رَضِيَ اللهُ عَنْهُ عَنْ رَسُولِ اللهِ صلى الله عليه وسلم قَالَ:

"إِنَّ اللهَ كَتَبَ الْإِحْسَانَ عَلَى كُلِّ شَيْءٍ، فَإِذَا قَتَلْتُمْ فَأَحْسِنُوا الْقِتْلَةَ، وَإِذَا ذَبَحْتُمْ فَأَحْسِنُوا الذِّبْحَةَ، وَلْيُحِدَّ أَحَدُكُمْ شَفْرَتَهُ، وَلْيُرِحْ ذَبِيحَتَهُ".

رَوَاهُ: [مُسْلِمٌ]

I.   The First Translation

On the authority of Abu Ya'la Shaddad bin Aws (may Allah be pleased with him), that the Messenger of Allah (peace be upon him) said:

"Verily Allah has prescribed ihsan (perfection) in all things. Thus if you kill, kill well; and if you slaughter, slaughter well. Let each one of you sharpen his blade and let him spare suffering to the animal he slaughters."

[Related by Muslim]

II. The Second Translation

Shaddaad ibn Aws, may Allaah be pleased with him, reported that Allaah's Messenger, sallallaahu `alayhi wa sallam, said:

"Allaah has written good conduct for everything. If one of you kills, they should do so in a good manner, and if one of you slaughters, they should do so in a good manner. One should sharpen their blade and comfort their sacrificial animal."

[Reported by Muslim (1955)]

III. The Third Translation

On the authority of Abū Ya'la, Shaddād bin Aus, that the Messenger of Allah (ﷺ) said:

"Indeed, Allah has decreed ihsān for all things. So when you kill, kill well; and when you slaughter, slaughter well. Let each one of you sharpen his blade, and let him spare suffering to the animal he slaughters."

[Narrated by Muslim]

عَنْ أَبِي ذَرٍّ جُنْدَبِ بْنِ جُنَادَةَ، وَأَبِي عَبْدِ الرَّحْمَنِ مُعَاذِ بْنِ جَبَلٍ رَضِيَ اللَّهُ عَنْهُمَا، عَنْ رَسُولِ اللَّهِ صلى الله عليه وسلم قَالَ:

"اتَّقِ اللَّهَ حَيْثُمَا كُنْت، وَأَتْبِعْ السَّيِّئَةَ الْحَسَنَةَ تَمْحُهَا، وَخَالِقْ النَّاسَ بِخُلُقٍ حَسَنٍ".

رَوَاهُ التِّرْمِذِيُّ [رقم:1987] وَقَالَ: حَدِيثٌ حَسَنٌ.

I. The First Translation

On the authority of Abu Dharr Jundub ibn Junadah, and Abu 'Abd-ir-Rahman Mu'adh bin Jabal (may Allah be pleased with them) that the Messenger of Allah (peace and blessing of Allah be upon him) said:

"Be conscious of Allah wherever you are. Follow the bad deed with a good one to erase it, and engage others with beautiful character."

[Related by Tirmidhi]

II. The Second Translation

Abu Tharr, may Allaah be pleased with him, and Mu`aath ibn Jabal, may Allaah be pleased with him, reported that the Messenger of Allaah, sallallaahu `alayhi wa sallam, said:

"Have Taqwa of Allaah wherever you are, follow an evil action with a good deed, and it will erase it, and treat people with good conduct."

[Reported by At-Tirmithi (1987)]

III. The Third Translation

On the authority of Abū Dharr, Jundub bin Junādah, and Abū ʿAbdur-Raḥmān, Muʿādh bin Jabal, that the Messenger of Allah (ﷺ) said:

"Fear Allah wherever you are and follow up a bad deed with a good one; it will wipe it out, and deal with people by good moral character."

[Narrated by at-Tirmidhi – ḥasan-ṣaḥeeḥ]

عَنْ عَبْدِ اللّٰهِ بْنِ عَبَّاسٍ رَضِيَ اللّٰهُ عَنْهُمَا قَالَ:

كُنْت خَلْفَ رَسُولِ اللّٰهِ صلى الله عليه وسلم يَوْمًا، فَقَالَ: يَا غُلَامُ! إِنِّي

أُعَلِّمُك كَلِمَاتٍ: احْفَظْ اللّٰهَ يَحْفَظْك، احْفَظْ اللّٰهَ تَجِدْهُ تُجَاهَك، إِذَا سَأَلْت

فَاسْأَلْ اللّٰهَ، وَإِذَا اسْتَعَنْت فَاسْتَعِنْ بِاللّٰهِ، وَاعْلَمْ أَنَّ الْأُمَّةَ لَوْ اجْتَمَعَتْ عَلَى أَنْ

يَنْفَعُوك بِشَيْءٍ لَمْ يَنْفَعُوك إِلَّا بِشَيْءٍ قَدْ كَتَبَهُ اللّٰهُ لَك، وَإِنِ اجْتَمَعُوا عَلَى أَنْ

يَضُرُّوك بِشَيْءٍ لَمْ يَضُرُّوك إِلَّا بِشَيْءٍ قَدْ كَتَبَهُ اللّٰهُ عَلَيْك؛ رُفِعَتْ الْأَقْلَامُ،

وَجَفَّتْ الصُّحُفُ.

رَوَاهُ التِّرْمِذِيُّ، وَقَالَ: حَدِيثٌ حَسَنٌ صَحِيحٌ.

I. The First Translation

Abu al-'Abbas 'Abdullah bin 'Abbas, may Allaah be pleased
with him, reports:

"One day I was riding (a horse/camel) behind the Prophet,
peace and blessings be upon him, when he said, 'Young man,
I will teach you some words. Be mindful of God, and He will
take care of you. Be mindful of Him, and you shall find Him
at your side. If you ask, ask of God. If you need help, seek it
from God. Know that if the whole world were to gather
together in order to help you, they would not be able to help
you except if God had written so. And if the whole world were

to gather together in order to harm you, they would not harm you except if God had written so. The pens have been lifted, and the pages are dry."

[Related by Tirmidhi]

II. The Second Translation

`Abdullaah ibn `Abbaas, may Allaah be pleased with him, said:

"I was riding behind the Prophet, sallallaahu 'alayhi wa sallam, and he said: 'O boy, I will teach you some phrases: Preserve Allaah and He will preserve you. Preserve Allaah and you will find Him at your side. If you ask, ask of Allaah, and if you seek help, seek it from Allaah. Know that if the entire Ummah wanted to benefit you, they would not be able to benefit you except in something Allaah The Almighty has written or you, and if they entirely wanted to harm you, they would not be able to harm you except in something Allaah The Almighty has written for you. The pens have been raised and the parchments have dried.'"

[Reported by At-Tirmithi (2516) and he ruled it as authentic.]

III. The Third Translation

On the authority of Abū ʿAbbās, ʿAbdullāh bin ʿAbbās, who said:

One day I was [mounted] behind the Prophet (ﷺ), and he said to me, "Young man, I will teach you words [of advice]: Keep Allah in mind – He will keep you from harm. Keep Allah in mind – you will find Him before you. When you ask, ask Allah; and when you seek help, seek it from Allah. Know that even if the [whole] nation assembled in order to benefit you with something, it could not benefit you except by something Allah had already decreed for you; and if they assembled in order to harm you with something, they could not harm you except with something Allah had already decreed upon you. The pens have been lifted, and the pages have dried."

[Narrated by at-Tirmidhi – ḥasan-ṣaḥeeḥ]

Hadeeth: 20 :الحديث

عَنْ أَبِي مَسْعُودٍ عُقْبَةَ بْنِ عَمْرِو الْأَنْصَارِيِّ الْبَدْرِيِّ رَضِيَ اللهُ عَنْهُ قَالَ: قَالَ

رَسُولُ اللهِ صلى الله عليه وسلم:

"إِنَّ مِمَّا أَدْرَكَ النَّاسُ مِنْ كَلَامِ النُّبُوَّةِ الْأُولَى: إِذَا لَمْ تَسْتَحِ فَاصْنَعْ مَا شِئْتَ".

رَوَاهُ: [الْبُخَارِيُّ].

I. The First Translation

Abu Mas'ud 'Uqbah bin 'Amr al-Ansari al-Badri may Allaah
be pleased with him, reported that the Messenger of Allah
sallallaahu 'alayhi wa sallam, said:

"The Messenger of Allah, peace be upon him, said: 'Among
the early prophetic teachings that have reached people is this:
if you do not feel shame, do what you wish."

[Related by Al- Bukhari]

II. The Second Translation

Abu Mas`ood Al-Badri, may Allaah be pleased with him,
reported that Allaah's Messenger, sallallaahu `alayhi wa
sallam, said:

"Some speech of the previous prophets which has reached the
people is: 'If you have no shame, do as you wish."

[Reported by Al-Bukhaari (3484).]

III. The Third Translation

On the authority of Abū Masʿūd ʿUqbah bin ʿAmr al-Anṣāri al-Badri, who said: The Messenger of Allah (ﷺ) said:

"Among that which people knew from the words of former prophecy is: When you feel no shame, then do whatever you wish."

[Narrated by al-Bukhāri]

عَنْ أَبِي عَمْرٍو وَقِيلَ: أَبِي عَمْرَةَ سُفْيَانَ بْنِ عَبْدِ اللّهِ رَضِيَ اللهُ عَنْهُ قَالَ:

"قُلْت: يَا رَسُولَ اللّهِ! قُلْ لِي فِي الْإِسْلَامِ قَوْلًا لَا أَسْأَلُ عَنْهُ أَحَدًا غَيْرَك؛

قَالَ: قُلْ: آمَنْت بِاللّهِ ثُمّ اسْتَقِمْ"

رَوَاهُ: [مُسْلِمٌ].

I. The First Translation

On the authority of Sufyan bin Abdullah (may Allah be pleased with him) who said:

"I said, 'O Messenger of Allah, tell me something about Islam which I can ask of no one but you.'

He (peace be upon him) said, 'Say "I believe in Allah" — and then be steadfast.'"

[Related by Muslim]

II. The Second Translation

Sufyaan ibn `Abdullaah, may Allaah be pleased with him, said: "I said: 'O Allaah's Messenger, tell me something about Islaam that I can ask none but you.'

He, sallallaahu `alayhi wa sallam, said: 'Say: 'I believe in Allaah,' then remain steadfast.'"

[Reported by Muslim (38).]

III. The Third Translation

On the authority of Abū ʿAmr – and he is also mentioned as Abū ʿAmrah – Sufyān bin ʿAbdullāh, who said:

I said, "O Messenger of Allah, tell me something about Islam which I will not [need to] ask anyone but you."

He said, "Say, 'I believe in Allah,' and then remain upright."

[Narrated by Muslim]

عَنْ أَبِي عَبْدِ اللهِ جَابِرِ بْنِ عَبْدِ اللهِ الْأَنْصَارِيِّ رَضِيَ اللَّهُ عَنْهُمَا: "أَنَّ رَجُلًا

سَأَلَ رَسُولَ اللهِ صلى الله عليه وسلم فَقَالَ:

أَرَأَيْت إِذَا صَلَّيْت الْمَكْتُوبَاتِ، وَصُمْت رَمَضَانَ، وَأَحْلَلْت الْحَلَالَ، وَحَرَّمْت

الْحَرَامَ، وَلَمْ أَزِدْ عَلَى ذَلِكَ شَيْئًا؛ أَأَدْخُلُ الْجَنَّةَ؟ قَالَ: نَعَمْ".

رَوَاهُ: [مُسْلِمٌ].

I. The First Translation

On the authority of Abu Abdullah Jabir bin Abdullah al-Ansari (may Allah be pleased with him):

A man questioned the Messenger of Allah (peace be upon him) and said:

"Do you think that if I perform the obligatory prayers, fast in Ramadan, treat as lawful that which is halal, and treat as forbidden that which is haram, and do not increase upon that [in voluntary good deeds], then I shall enter Paradise?"

He (peace be upon him) replied, "Yes."

[Related by Muslim]

II. The Second Translation

Jaabir, may Allaah be pleased with him, reported that a man asked the Messenger of Allaah, sallallaahu `alayhi wa sallam:

"If I were to pray the obligatory prayers, fast Ramadhaan, perform the lawful, and avoid the unlawful, without increasing anything on that, would I enter Paradise?"

The Prophet, sallallaahu `alayhi wa sallam, said: "Yes." The man said: "By Allaah, I will not add anything to that."

He said: "Perform the lawful and avoid the unlawful."

[Reported by Muslim (15).]

III. The Third Translation

On the authority of Abū `Abdullāh, Jābir bin `Abdullāh al-Anṣāri: A man asked the Messenger of Allah (ﷺ), "Do you consider: if I prayed the obligatory prayers, fasted Ramadhān, allowed what is lawful and prohibited what is unlawful and added nothing to that, I would enter Paradise?" He said, "Yes."

[Narrated by Muslim]

عَنْ أَبِي مَالِكٍ الْحَارِثِ بنِ عَاصِمٍ الْأَشْعَرِيّ رَضِيَ اللهُ عَنْهُ قَالَ: قَالَ رَسُولُ اللهِ صلى الله عليه وسلم:

"الطَّهُورُ شَطْرُ الْإِيمَانِ، وَالْحَمْدُ لِلّهِ تَمْلَأُ الْمِيزَانَ، وَسُبْحَانَ اللهِ وَالْحَمْدُ لِلّهِ تَمْلَآنِ -أَوْ: تَمْلَأُ- مَا بَيْنَ السَّمَاءِ وَالْأَرْضِ، وَالصَّلَاةُ نُورٌ، وَالصَّدَقَةُ بُرْهَانٌ، وَالصَّبْرُ ضِيَاءٌ، وَالْقُرْآنُ حُجَّةٌ لَكَ أَوْ عَلَيْكَ، كُلُّ النَّاسِ يَغْدُو، فَبَائِعٌ نَفْسَهُ فَمُعْتِقُهَا أَوْ مُوبِقُهَا".

رَوَاهُ: [مُسْلِمٌ].

I.   The First Translation

On the authority of Abu Malik al-Harith bin Asim al-Ashari (may Allah be pleased with him) who said: The Messenger of Allah (peace be upon him) said:

"Purity is half of Iman. Alhamdulillah (praise be to Allah) fills the scales, and subhan-Allah (how far from imperfection is Allah) and Alhamdulillah (praise be to Allah) fill that which is between heaven and earth. And the Salah (prayer) is a light, and charity is a proof, and patience is illumination, and the Qur'an is a proof either for you or against you. Every person starts his day as a vendor of his soul, either freeing it or bringing about its ruin."

[Related by Muslim]

II. The Second Translation

Abu Maalik Al-Ash'ari, may Allaah be pleased with him, said that Allaah's Messenger, sallallaahu 'alayhi wa sallam, said:

"Purity is half of faith, Al-Hamdu Lillaah [All praise is for Allaah] fills the scale, and Subhaana Allaah wal-Hamdu Lillaah [Transcendent is Allaah and all praise is for Allaah] fills what is between the heavens and the earth. Prayer is a light, charity is evidence, patience is illumination, and the Qur'aan is either a proof for or against you. Every person departs and sells their soul, and they either ransom it or put it into perdition."

[Reported by Muslim (223).]

III. The Third Translation

On the authority of Abū Mālik, al-Ḥārith bin 'Aasim al-Ash'ari, who said: The Messenger of Allah (ﷺ) said:

"Purity is half the faith. And 'al-ḥamdu lillāh' fills the scale; and 'subḥān Allāh' and 'al-ḥamdu lilāah' fill what is between the heaven and earth. Prayer is light, ṣadaqah is evidence, patience is burning light, and the Qur'ān is an argument for you or against you. Each of the people begins at morning, selling his soul – either freeing it [thereby] or destroying it."

[Narrated by Muslim]

عَنْ أَبِي ذَرٍّ الْغِفَارِيِّ رَضِيَ اللهُ عَنْهُ عَنِ النَّبِيِّ صلى الله عليه وسلم فِيمَا يَرْوِيهِ عَنْ رَبِّهِ تَبَارَكَ وَتَعَالَى، أَنَّهُ قَالَ:

"يَا عِبَادِي: إِنِّي حَرَّمْت الظُّلْمَ عَلَى نَفْسِي، وَجَعَلْته بَيْنَكُمْ مُحَرَّمًا؛ فَلَا تَظَالَمُوا. يَا عِبَادِي! كُلُّكُمْ ضَالٌّ إِلَّا مَنْ هَدَيْته، فَاسْتَهْدُونِي أَهْدِكُمْ. يَا عِبَادِي! كُلُّكُمْ جَائِعٌ إِلَّا مَنْ أَطْعَمْته، فَاسْتَطْعِمُونِي أُطْعِمْكُمْ. يَا عِبَادِي! كُلُّكُمْ عَارٍ إِلَّا مَنْ كَسَوْته، فَاسْتَكْسُونِي أَكْسُكُمْ. يَا عِبَادِي! إِنَّكُمْ تُخْطِئُونَ بِاللَّيْلِ وَالنَّهَارِ، وَأَنَا أَغْفِرُ الذُّنُوبَ جَمِيعًا؛ فَاسْتَغْفِرُونِي أَغْفِرْ لَكُمْ. يَا عِبَادِي! إِنَّكُمْ لَنْ تَبْلُغُوا ضُرِّي فَتَضُرُّونِي، وَلَنْ تَبْلُغُوا نَفْعِي فَتَنْفَعُونِي. يَا عِبَادِي! لَوْ أَنَّ أَوَّلَكُمْ وَآخِرَكُمْ وَإِنْسَكُمْ وَجِنَّكُمْ كَانُوا عَلَى أَتْقَى قَلْبِ رَجُلٍ وَاحِدٍ مِنْكُمْ، مَا زَادَ ذَلِكَ فِي مُلْكِي شَيْئًا. يَا عِبَادِي! لَوْ أَنَّ أَوَّلَكُمْ وَآخِرَكُمْ وَإِنْسَكُمْ وَجِنَّكُمْ كَانُوا عَلَى أَفْجَرِ قَلْبِ رَجُلٍ وَاحِدٍ مِنْكُمْ، مَا نَقَصَ ذَلِكَ مِنْ مُلْكِي شَيْئًا. يَا عِبَادِي! لَوْ أَنَّ أَوَّلَكُمْ وَآخِرَكُمْ وَإِنْسَكُمْ وَجِنَّكُمْ قَامُوا فِي صَعِيدٍ وَاحِدٍ، فَسَأَلُونِي، فَأَعْطَيْت كُلَّ وَاحِدٍ مَسْأَلَته، مَا نَقَصَ ذَلِكَ مِمَّا عِنْدِي إِلَّا كَمَا يَنْقُصُ الْمِخْيَطُ إِذَا أُدْخِلَ الْبَحْرَ. يَا عِبَادِي! إِنَّمَا هِيَ أَعْمَالُكُمْ أُحْصِيهَا لَكُمْ، ثُمَّ أُوَفِّيكُمْ إِيَّاهَا؛ فَمَنْ وَجَدَ خَيْرًا فَلْيَحْمَدْ اللَّهَ، وَمَنْ وَجَدَ غَيْرَ ذَلِكَ فَلَا يَلُومَن إِلَّا نَفْسَهُ".

رَوَاهُ: [مُسْلِمٌ].

I.   The First Translation

On the authority of Abu Dharr Al-Ghafari, of the Prophet (peace be upon him) is that among the sayings he relates from his Lord is that He said:

"O My servants! I have forbidden oppression for Myself, and I have made it forbidden amongst you, so do not oppress one another. O My servants, all of you are astray except those whom I have guided, so seek guidance from Me and I shall guide you. O My servants, all of you are hungry except those whom I have fed, so seek food from Me and I shall feed you. O My servants, all of you are naked except those whom I have clothed, so seek clothing from Me and I shall clothe you. O My servants, you sommit sins by day and by night, and I forgive all sins, so seek forgiveness from Me and I shall forgive you. O My servants, you will not attain harming Me so as to harm Me, and you will not attain benefitting Me so as to benefit Me. O My servants, if the first of you and the last of you, and the humans of you and the jinn of you, were all as pious as the most pious heart of any individual amongst you, then this would not increase My Kingdom an iota. O My servants, if the first of you and the last of you, and the humans of you and the jinn of you, were all as wicked as the most wicked heart of any individual amongst you, then this would not decrease My Kingdom an iota. O My servants, if the first of you and the last of you, and the humans of you and the jinn of you, were all to stand together in one place and ask of Me, and I were to give everyone what he requested, then that would not decrease what I Possess, except what is decreased of the ocean when a needle is dipped into it. O My servants, it is but your deeds that I account for you, and then recompense you for. So he who finds good, let him praise Allah, and he who finds other than that, let him blame no one but himself."

[Related by Muslim (2577)]

II. The Second Translation

On the authority of Abū Dharr al-Ghifāri from the Prophet ( ) among that which he related from his Lord, the Mighty and Majestic, is that He said:

"O My servants, indeed I have prohibited injustice for Myself and made it among you prohibited, so be not unjust to one another. O My servants, all of you are lost except whom I have guided, so seek guidance from Me and I will guide you. O My servants, all of you are hungry except whom I have fed, so ask Me for food and I will feed you. O My servants, all of you are naked except whom I have clothed, so ask Me for clothing and I will clothe you. O My servants, indeed you err by night and by day and I forgive all sins, so seek forgiveness of Me and I will forgive you. O My servants, never will you reach [so far as] to harm Me so you could harm Me, and never will you reach [so far as] to benefit Me so you could benefit Me. O My servants, if the first of you, the last of you, the humans of you, and the jinn of you were [all] as righteous as the most righteous heart of one man among you, it would not increase My dominion at all.

O My servants, if the first of you, the last of you, the humans of you, and the jinn of you were as wicked as the most wicked heart of one man among you, it would not decrease My dominion at all. O My servants, if the first of you, the last of you, the humans of you, and the jinn of you were to stand in one place and ask something of Me and I gave each one his request, that would not decrease what I have except like the needle decreases [the water] when put into the sea. O My servants, it is only your deeds I enumerate for you and then I fully compensate you for them. So whoever finds good – let him praise Allah, and whoever finds otherwise should certainly not blame except himself."

[Narrated by Muslim]

عَنْ أَبِي ذَرٍّ رَضِيَ اللهُ عَنْهُ:

"نَاسًا مِنْ أَصْحَابِ رَسُولِ اللهِ صلى الله عليه وسلم قَالُوا لِلنَّبِيِّ صلى الله عليه وسلم يَا رَسُولَ اللهِ ذَهَبَ أَهْلُ الدُّثُورِ بِالْأُجُورِ؛ يُصَلُّونَ كَمَا نُصَلِّي، وَيَصُومُونَ كَمَا نَصُومُ، وَيَتَصَدَّقُونَ بِفُضُولِ أَمْوَالِهِمْ.

قَالَ: أَوَلَيْسَ قَدْ جَعَلَ اللهُ لَكُمْ مَا تَصَدَّقُونَ؟ إِنَّ بِكُلِّ تَسْبِيحَةٍ صَدَقَةً، وَكُلِّ تَكْبِيرَةٍ صَدَقَةً، وَكُلِّ تَحْمِيدَةٍ صَدَقَةً، وَكُلِّ تَهْلِيلَةٍ صَدَقَةً، وَأَمْرٌ بِمَعْرُوفٍ صَدَقَةٌ، وَنَهْيٌ عَنْ مُنْكَرٍ صَدَقَةٌ، وَفِي بُضْعِ أَحَدِكُمْ صَدَقَةٌ.

قَالُوا: يَا رَسُولَ اللهِ أَيَأْتِي أَحَدُنَا شَهْوَتَهُ وَيَكُونُ لَهُ فِيهَا أَجْرٌ؟

قَالَ: أَرَأَيْتُمْ لَوْ وَضَعَهَا فِي حَرَامٍ أَكَانَ عَلَيْهِ وِزْرٌ؟ فَكَذَلِكَ إِذَا وَضَعَهَا فِي الْحَلَالِ، كَانَ لَهُ أَجْرٌ".

رَوَاهُ: [مُسْلِمٌ].

I.   The First Translation

On the authority of Abu Dharr (may Allah be pleased with him):

"Some people from amongst the Companions of the Messenger of Allah (peace be upon him) said to the Prophet (peace be upon him), 'O Messenger of Allah, the affluent have made off with the rewards; they pray as we pray, they fast as we fast, and they give [much] in charity by virtue of their wealth.'

He (peace be upon him) said, 'Has not Allah made things for you to give in charity? Truly every tasbeehah [saying subhan-Allah] is a charity, and every takbeerah [saying Allahu akbar] is a charity, and every tahmeedah [saying alhamdulillah] is a charity, and every tahleelah [saying la ilaha illAllah] is a charity. And commanding the good is a charity, and forbidding an evil is a charity, and in the sexual act of each one of you there is a charity.'

They said, 'O Messenger of Allah, when one of us fulfills his sexual desire, will he have some reward for that?'

He (peace be upon him) said: 'Do you not see that if he were to act upon it [his desire] in an unlawful manner, then he would be deserving of punishment? Likewise, if he were to act upon it in a lawful manner, then he will be deserving of a reward.'"

[Related by Muslim]

II. The Second Translation

Abu Tharr, may Allaah be pleased with him, reported that some people from the Companions of the Prophet, sallallaahu `alayhi wa sallam, said to him: "O Allaah's Messenger, those with wealth have taken all the rewards. They pray as we do, fast as we do, but give the excess wealth they possess in charity."

The Prophet, sallallaahu `alayhi wa sallam, said: "Has not Allaah the Exalted given you a means to give charity? Every time you make Tasbeeh [i.e. say, 'Subhaan Allaah'] , it is a charity, every time you make Takbeer [i.e. say, 'Allaahu Akbar'] it is a charity, every time you make Tahmeed [i.e. say, 'Al-Hamdu Lillaah'] it is a charity, every time you make Tahleel [i.e. say, 'La ilaaha illallaah'] it is a charity, every time you order good it is a charity, every time you forbid evil it is a charity, and when you have intercourse it is a charity."

They said: "O Allaah's Messenger, if one of us fulfills their desires, would they get rewarded for that?"

He, sallallaahu `alayhi wa sallam, said: "Do you see if they were to satisfy their desires in an unlawful way, would they have a burden due to that? Likewise, if they satisfy it in a lawful way, they would be rewarded for it."

[Reported by Muslim (1006).]

III. The Third Translation

Also on the authority of Abū Dharr: Some of the companions of the Messenger of Allah said to the Prophet (ﷺ): "O Messenger of Allah, the affluent have taken the rewards: they pray as we pray, they fast as we fast, and they give in charity the excess of their wealth."

He said, "Has not Allah made something for you to do in charity? Indeed, in each saying of 'subḥān Allāh' is a charity, and each 'Allāhu akbar' is a charity, and each 'al-ḥamdulillāh' is a charity, and each 'lā ilāha ill-Allāh' is a charity, and enjoining what is right is a charity, and prohibiting what is wrong is a charity, and in the sexual intercourse of one of you is a charity."

They said, "O Messenger of Allah, does one of us indulge in his desire and get for it a reward?"

He said, "Have you considered: if he were to do it unlawfully, would he have for it a burden [of sin]? Similarly, when he does it lawfully, he will have for it a reward."

[Narrated by Muslim]

عَنْ أَبِي هُرَيْرَةَ رَضِيَ اللهُ عَنْهُ قَالَ: قَالَ رَسُولُ اللهِ صلى الله عليه وسلم:

"كُلُّ سُلَامَى مِنَ النَّاسِ عَلَيْهِ صَدَقَةٌ، كُلَّ يَوْمٍ تَطْلُعُ فِيهِ الشَّمْسُ تَعْدِلُ بَيْنَ

اثْنَيْنِ صَدَقَةٌ، وَتُعِينُ الرَّجُلَ فِي دَابَّتِهِ فَتَحْمِلُهُ عَلَيْهَا أَوْ تَرْفَعُ لَهُ عَلَيْهَا مَتَاعَهُ

صَدَقَةٌ، وَالْكَلِمَةُ الطَّيِّبَةُ صَدَقَةٌ، وَبِكُلِّ خُطْوَةٍ تَمْشِيهَا إِلَى الصَّلَاةِ صَدَقَةٌ،

وَتُمِيطُ الْأَذَى عَنِ الطَّرِيقِ صَدَقَةٌ".

رَوَاهُ: [الْبُخَارِيُّ] وَ [مُسْلِمٌ].

I.   The First Translation

Abu Hurairah (may Allah be pleased with him) reported that the Messenger of Allah (peace be upon him) said,

"Every joint of a person must perform a charity each day that the sun rises: to judge justly between two people is a charity. To help a man with his mount, lifting him onto it or hoisting up his belongings onto it, is a charity. And the good word is a charity. And every step that you take towards the prayer is a charity, and removing a harmful object from the road is a charity."

[Related by Al-Bukhaari (2989) and Muslim (1009)]

II. The Second Translation

On the authority of Abū Hurayrah, who said: The Messenger of Allah (ﷺ) said:

"Upon the people's every joint a charity is due each day the sun rises. Your being just between two persons is a charity; your helping a man with his mount, lifting him onto it or hoisting up his belongings onto it for him is a charity; and a good word is a charity. And with each step you take walking to the [congregational] prayer is a charity; and your removing something harmful from the road is a charity."

[Narrated by al-Bukhāri and Muslim]

عَنْ النَّوَاسِ بْنِ سَمْعَانَ رَضِيَ اللهُ عَنْهُ عَنْ النَّبِيّ صلى الله عليه وسلم قَالَ:

"الْبِرُ حُسْنُ الْخُلُقِ، وَالْإِثْمُ مَا حَاكَ فِي صَدْرِك، وَكَرِهْتَ أَنْ يَطَّلِعَ عَلَيْهِ النَّاسُ"

رَوَاهُ: [مُسْلِمٌ].

وَعَنْ وَابِصَةَ بْنِ مَعْبَدٍ رَضِيَ اللهُ عَنْهُ قَالَ:

أَتَيْت رَسُولَ اللهِ صلى الله عليه وسلم فَقَالَ: "جِئْتَ تَسْأَلُ عَنْ الْبِرِّ؟ قُلْت:

نَعَمْ. فقَالَ: استفت قلبك، الْبِرُّ مَا اطْمَأَنَّتْ إِلَيْهِ النَّفْسُ، وَاطْمَأَنَّ إِلَيْهِ الْقَلْبُ،

وَالْإِثْمُ مَا حَاكَ فِي النَّفْسِ وَتَرَدَّدَ فِي الصَّدْرِ، وَإِنْ أَفْتَاكَ النَّاسُ وَأَفْتَوْكَ" .

[حَدِيثٌ حَسَنٌ، رَوَيْنَاهُ فِي مُسْنَدَي الْإِمَامَيْنِ

أَحْمَدَ بْنِ حَنْبَلٍ، وَالدَّارِمِيّ ، بِإِسْنَادٍ حَسَنٍ.].

I.   The First Translation

On the authority of an-Nawas bin Sam'an (may Allah be pleased with him), the Prophet (peace be upon him) said:

"Righteousness is in good character, and wrongdoing is that which wavers in your soul, and which you dislike people finding out about."

[Related by Muslim]

And on the authority of Wabisah bin Ma'bad (may Allah be pleased with him) who said,

"I came to the Messenger of Allah (peace be upon him) and he (peace be upon him) said, 'You have come to ask about righteousness.' I said, 'Yes.' He (peace be upon him) said, 'Consult your heart. Righteousness is that about which the soul feels at ease and the heart feels tranquil. And wrongdoing is that which wavers in the soul and causes uneasiness in the breast, even though people have repeatedly given their legal opinion [in its favour].'"

[A good hadeeth transmitted from the musnads of the two imams, Ahmed bin Hambal and Al-Darimi]

II. The Second Translation

An-Nawwaas ibn Sam`aan, may Allaah be pleased with him, reported that the Prophet, sallallaahu `alayhi wa sallam, said: "Piety is having good character, and sin is the action that disturbs you and you dislike people seeing you do."

[Reported by Muslim (2553)]

Waabisah ibn Ma`bad, may Allaah be pleased with him, said: "I went to Allaah's Messenger, sallallaahu `alayhi wa sallam, and he said: 'Have you come to ask about piety and sin?' I said: 'Yes.' He, sallallaahu `alayhi wa sallam, said: 'Ask your heart. Piety is what your soul feels tranquil doing and the heart feels serene, and sin is what disturbs your soul and causes your chest to hesitate, even if people continuously give you rulings [that it is permissible]."'

[Reported by Ahmad (18001)]

III. The Third Translation

On the authority of an-Nawwās bin Samʿān that the Prophet (ﷺ) said: "Righteousness is good morals, and wrongdoing is that which wavers within yourself and you would dislike people to discover."

[Narrated by Muslim]

On the authority of Wābiṣah bin Maʿbad, who said:

I came to the Messenger of Allah (ﷺ), and he said, "You have come to ask about righteousness?" I said, "Yes." He said, "Consult your heart. Righteousness is that with which the self is assured and the heart is assured, and wrongdoing is that which wavers within the self and falters in the breast, even if the people have given you a ruling and gave you a ruling [again]."

[Narrated in the Musnads of the two Imāms,
Aḥmad bin Ḥanbal and ad-Dārimi - ḥasan]

عَنْ أَبِي نَجِيحٍ الْعِرْبَاضِ بْنِ سَارِيَةَ رَضِيَ اللهُ عَنْهُ قَالَ:

"وَعَظَنَا رَسُولُ اللهِ صلى الله عليه وسلم مَوْعِظَةً وَجِلَتْ مِنْهَا الْقُلُوبُ، وَذَرَفَتْ مِنْهَا الْعُيُونُ، فَقُلْنَا: يَا رَسُولَ اللهِ! كَأَنَّهَا مَوْعِظَةُ مُوَدِّعٍ فَأَوْصِنَا، قَالَ: أُوصِيكُمْ بِتَقْوَى اللهِ، وَالسَّمْعِ وَالطَّاعَةِ وَإِنْ تَأَمَّرَ عَلَيْكُمْ عَبْدٌ، فَإِنَّهُ مَنْ يَعِشْ مِنْكُمْ فَسَيَرَى اخْتِلَافًا كَثِيرًا، فَعَلَيْكُمْ بِسُنَّتِي وَسُنَّةِ الْخُلَفَاءِ الرَّاشِدِينَ الْمَهْدِيِّينَ، عَضُّوا عَلَيْهَا بِالنَّوَاجِذِ، وَإِيَّاكُمْ وَمُحْدَثَاتِ الْأُمُورِ؛ فَإِنَّ كُلَّ بِدْعَةٍ ضَلَالَةٌ".

رَوَاهُ: [أَبُو دَاوُدَ، وَالتِّرْمِذِيُّ، وَقَالَ: حَدِيثٌ حَسَنٌ صَحِيحٌ.].

I. The First Translation

It was narrated on the authority of Abu Najih al-Irbad bin Sariyah (may Allah be pleased with him) who said:

"The Messenger of Allah (peace be upon him) delivered an admonition that made our hearts fearful and our eyes tearful. We said, "O Messenger of Allah, it is as if this were a farewell sermon, so advise us." He said, "I enjoin you to have Taqwa of Allah and that you listen and obey, even if a slave is made a ruler over you. He among you who lives long enough will see many differences. So for you is to observe my Sunnah and the Sunnah of the rightly-principled and rightly-guided successors, holding on to them with your molar teeth. Beware of newly-introduced matters, for every innovation (bid'ah) is an error."

[Related by Abu Dawud & Al-Tirmidhi,
who says it is an authentic hadith - hasan saheeh]

II. The Second Translation

Al-`Irbaadh ibn Saariyah, may Allaah be pleased with him, said:

"Allaah's Messenger, sallallaahu `alayhi wa sallam, gave us an eloquent admonition which caused the eyes to shed tears and the hearts to become afraid. Someone then said: 'This is the admonition of someone who will soon part. What do you charge us with doing?' He, sallallaahu `alayhi wa sallam, said: 'I advise you to fear Allaah and to hear and obey, even if an Ethiopian slave were placed in charge of you. Any of you who live after me will see much differing. Beware of newly invented matters, because they are misguided. Any of you who lives to reach those matters should hold fast to my Sunnah and that of the rightly guided Caliphs. Bite onto it with your molar teeth.'"

[Reported by At-Tirmithi (2676)]

III. The Third Translation

On the authority of Abū Najeeḥ al-'Irbādh bin Sāriyah, who said:

The Messenger of Allah (ﷺ) admonished us with a warning from which [our] hearts became fearful and [our] eyes shed tears. So we said, "O Messenger of Allah (ﷺ), it is as if it was a final warning, so instruct us." He said, "I direct you to fear Allah, the Mighty and Majestic, and to hear and obey, even if a slave is made a leader over you. For indeed, he who lives long among you will see much controversy. So you must adhere to my sunnah and the sunnah of the rightly guided caliphs; clench it with your molar teeth. And beware of newly devised matters, for every newly devised thing is an innovation, and every innovation is misguidance, and every misguidance is in the Fire."

[Narrated by Abū Dāwūd and at-Tirmidhi who graded it ḥasan-ṣaḥeeḥ]

عَنْ مُعَاذِ بْنِ جَبَلٍ رَضِيَ اللهُ عَنْهُ قَالَ:

قُلْت يَا رَسُولَ اللهِ! أَخْبِرْنِي بِعَمَلٍ يُدْخِلُنِي الْجَنَّةَ وَيُبَاعِدْنِي مِنْ النَّارِ.

قَالَ: "لَقَدْ سَأَلْت عَنْ عَظِيمٍ، وَإِنَّهُ لَيَسِيرٌ عَلَى مَنْ يَسَّرَهُ اللهُ عَلَيْهِ: تَعْبُدُ اللهَ

لَا تُشْرِكُ بِهِ شَيْئًا، وَتُقِيمُ الصَّلَاةَ، وَتُؤْتِي الزَّكَاةَ، وَتَصُومُ رَمَضَانَ، وَتَحُجُّ الْبَيْتَ،

ثُمَّ قَالَ: أَلَا أَدُلُّك عَلَى أَبْوَابِ الْخَيْرِ؟ الصَّوْمُ جُنَّةٌ، وَالصَّدَقَةُ تُطْفِئُ الْخَطِيئَةَ

كَمَا يُطْفِئُ الْمَاءُ النَّارَ، وَصَلَاةُ الرَّجُلِ فِي جَوْفِ اللَّيْلِ، ثُمَّ تَلَا:

﴿ تَتَجَافَىٰ جُنُوبُهُمْ عَنِ ٱلْمَضَاجِعِ يَدْعُونَ رَبَّهُمْ خَوْفًا وَطَمَعًا وَمِمَّا

رَزَقْنَٰهُمْ يُنفِقُونَ ۝ فَلَا تَعْلَمُ نَفْسٌ مَّا أُخْفِىَ لَهُم مِّن قُرَّةِ أَعْيُنٍ جَزَآءً

بِمَا كَانُوا۟ يَعْمَلُونَ ۝ ﴾ (سورة السجدة)

ثُمَّ قَالَ: أَلَا أُخْبِرُك بِرَأْسِ الْأَمْرِ وَعَمُودِهِ وَذُرْوَةِ سَنَامِهِ؟ قُلْت: بَلَى يَا رَسُولَ

اللهِ. قَالَ: رَأْسُ الْأَمْرِ الْإِسْلَامُ، وَعَمُودُهُ الصَّلَاةُ، وَذُرْوَةُ سَنَامِهِ الْجِهَادُ، ثُمَّ

قَالَ: أَلَا أُخْبِرُك بِمَلَاكِ ذَلِكَ كُلِّهِ؟ فَقُلْت: بَلَى يَا رَسُولَ اللهِ ! فَأَخَذَ بِلِسَانِهِ

وَقَالَ: كُفَّ عَلَيْك هَذَا. قُلْت: يَا نَبِيَّ اللهِ وَإِنَّا لَمُؤَاخَذُونَ بِمَا نَتَكَلَّمُ بِهِ؟ فَقَالَ:

ثَكِلَتْك أُمُّك وَهَلْ يَكُبُّ النَّاسَ عَلَى وُجُوهِهِمْ -أَوْ قَالَ عَلَى مَنَاخِرِهِمْ- إِلَّا

حَصَائِدُ أَلْسِنَتِهِمْ؟!".

[رَوَاهُ التِّرْمِذِيُّ، وَقَالَ: حَدِيثٌ حَسَنٌ صَحِيحٌ.]

I.   The First Translation

On the authority of Muadh bin Jabal (may Allah be please with him) who said:

I said, 'O Messenger of Allah, tell me of an act which will take me into Paradise and will keep me away from the Hellfire.' He (peace be upon him) said, 'You have asked me about a great matter, yet it is easy for him for whom Allah makes it easy. Worship Allah without associating any partners with Him; establish the prayer; pay the Zakah; fast in Ramadan; and make the pilgrimage to the House.'

"Then he (peace be upon him) said, 'Shall I not guide you towards the means of goodness? Fasting is a shield, charity wipes away sin as water extinguishes fire, and the praying of a man in the depths of the night.' Then he (peace be upon him) recited:

'[Those] who forsake their beds, to invoke their Lord in fear and hope, and they spend (charity in Allah's cause) out of what We have bestowed on them. No person knows what is kept hidden for them of joy as a reward for what they used to do' [as-Sajdah, 16-17].

"Then he (peace be upon him) said, 'Shall I not inform you of the head of the matter, its pillar and its peak?' I said, 'Yes, O

Messenger of Allah.' He (peace be upon him) said, 'The head of the matter is Islam, its pillar is the prayer and its peak is jihad.' Then he (peace be upon him) said, 'Shall I not tell you of the foundation of all of that?' I said, 'Yes, O Messenger of Allah.' So he took hold of his tongue and said, 'Restrain this.' I said, 'O Prophet of Allah, will we be taken to account for what we say with it?' He (peace be upon him) said, 'May your mother be bereaved of you, O Muadh! Is there anything that throws people into the Hellfire upon their faces, or on their noses, except the harvests of their tongues?'

[Related by Tirmidhi]

II. The Second Translation

Mu`aath ibn Jabal, may Allaah be pleased with him, said:

"I was with the Prophet, sallallaahu `alayhi wa sallam, while traveling, and one day, I was close to him while we were treading, so I said: 'O Allaah's Messenger, sallallaahu `alayhi wa sallam, tell me of an action which would cause me to enter Paradise and would create a distance between myself and the Hellfire.'

He, sallallaahu `alayhi wa sallam, said: 'You have asked me about a great matter, and it is easy on those whom Allaah the Exalted makes it easy for. Worship Allaah the Exalted without associating anything in worship with Him, establish the prayers, give obligatory charity, fast Ramadhaan, and perform Hajj.' Then he, sallallaahu `alayhi wa sallam, said: 'Shall I not guide you to the doors of goodness: Fasting is a protection, charity extinguishes mistakes just as water extinguishes fire, and prayer by a person during the middle of the night.'" Then, he, sallallaahu `alayhi wa sallam, recited:

﴿ تَتَجَافَىٰ جُنُوبُهُمْ عَنِ ٱلْمَضَاجِعِ يَدْعُونَ رَبَّهُمْ خَوْفًا وَطَمَعًا وَمِمَّا رَزَقْنَٰهُمْ يُنفِقُونَ ۝ فَلَا تَعْلَمُ نَفْسٌ مَّآ أُخْفِىَ لَهُم مِّن قُرَّةِ أَعْيُنٍ جَزَآءً بِمَا كَانُوا۟ يَعْمَلُونَ ۝ ﴾ (سورة السجدة: 16-17)

{They arise from [their] beds; they supplicate their Lord in fear and aspiration, and from what We have provided them, they spend. And no soul knows what has been hidden for them of comfort for eyes as reward for what they used to do.} [QUR'AAN 32: 16-17]

Then, he, sallallaahu `alayhi wa sallam, said: "Shall I not inform you of the head of the matter, its pillar, and its peak?" Mu`aath, may Allaah be pleased with him, said: "Yes, O Allaah's Messenger." He, sallallaahu `alayhi wa sallam, said: "The head of the matter is Islam, its pillar is prayer, and its peak is Jihaad." Then he, sallallaahu `alayhi wa sallam, said: "Shall I not tell you of the foundation of all that?" Mu`aath, may Allaah be pleased with him, said: "Yes, O Allaah's Prophet." He, sallallaahu `alayhi wa sallam, then took his tongue and said: "Refrain from this." Mu`aath, may Allaah be pleased with him, said: "O Prophet of Allaah, are we held accountable for what we utter?" The Prophet, sallallaahu `alayhi wa sallam, said: "May your mother lose you, O Mu`aath! Is there anything that throws people into the Hellfire upon their faces or on their noses except the harvests of their tongues?"

[Reported by At-Tirmithi (2616) and he ruled it as authentic]

III. The Third Translation

On the authority of Mu'ādh bin Jabal, who said: I said, "O Messenger of Allah (ﷺ), inform me of a deed which will take me into Paradise and keep me away from the Fire."

He said, "You have asked me about a tremendous matter, but indeed, it is easy for one for whom Allah, the Exalted, makes it easy. You should worship Allah, associating nothing with Him, establish prayer, fast [the month of] Ramadhān, and make the pilgrimage to the House."

Then he said, "Shall I not point out to you the gates of goodness? Fasting is a shield. Charity extinguishes sin as water extinguishes fire and [so does] the prayer of a man in the middle of the night." Then he recited:

"They forsake their beds, invoking their Lord in fear and hope, and spend of that We have provided them. And no soul knows what has been hidden for them of satisfaction as reward for what they used to do."

Then he said, "Shall I not inform you of the head of the matter, its pillar and the peak of its elevation?"

I said, "Yes, O Messenger of Allah."

He said, "The head of the matter is islām [i.e., submission], its pillar is prayer, and the peak of its elevation is jihād." Then he said, "Shall I not inform you of the foundation of all that?"

I said, "Yes, O Messenger of Allah."

So he took hold of his tongue and said, "Restrain this."

I said, "O Prophet of Allah, will we be blamed for what we talk about?"

He said, "May your mother be bereaved of you, O Muʿādh! Does anything topple people into the Fire on their faces" or he said, "on their noses except the harvests of their tongues?"

[Narrated by at-Tirmidhi, who said it was ḥasan-ṣaheeḥ]

Hadeeth: 30 الحديث:

عَنْ أَبِي ثَعْلَبَةَ الْخُشَنِيِّ جُرْثُومِ بن نَاشِرٍ رَضِيَ اللهُ عَنْهُ عَنْ رَسُولِ اللهِ صلى الله عليه وسلم قال:

"إِنَّ اللَّهَ تَعَالَى فَرَضَ فَرَائِضَ فَلَا تُضَيِّعُوهَا، وَحَدَّ حُدُودًا فَلَا تَعْتَدُوهَا، وَحَرَّمَ أَشْيَاءَ فَلَا تَنْتَهِكُوهَا، وَسَكَتَ عَنْ أَشْيَاءَ رَحْمَةً لَكُمْ غَيْرَ نِسْيَانٍ فَلَا تَبْحَثُوا عَنْهَا".

[حَدِيثٌ حَسَنٌ، رَوَاهُ الدَّارَقُطْنِيُّ "في سننه"، وَغَيْرُهُ.].

I.   The First Translation

On the authority of Jurthum bin Nashir (may Allah be pleased with him) that the Messenger of Allah (peace be upon him) said:

Verily Allah the Almighty has laid down religious obligations (fara'id), so do not neglect them. He has set boundaries, so do not overstep them. He has prohibited some things, so do not violate them; about some things He was silent, out of compassion for you, not forgetfulness, so seek not after them.

[Related by Daraqutni]

II. The Second Translation

Abu Tha`labah Al-Khushani, may Allaah be pleased with him, reported that Allaah's Messenger, sallallaahu `alayhi wa sallam, said:

"Allaah the Exalted has obligated the obligations, so do not neglect them. He has forbidden the prohibitions, so do not fall into them. He has set limits, so do not transgress them. Also, He has remained silent about other things, not out of forgetfulness, so do not ask about them."

[Reported by Ad-Daaraqutni in his book Sunan Ad-Daaraqutni (4396)]

III. The Third Translation

On the authority of Abū Tha'labah al-Khushani, Jurthūm bin Nāshir, that the Messenger of Allah (ﷺ) said:

"Indeed, Allah, the Exalted, has imposed [religious] obligations, so do not neglect them. And He has set limits, so do not overstep them. And He has prohibited things, so do not violate them. And He has kept silent about [certain] things out of mercy to you, not forgetfulness, so do not search them out."

[Hadīth ḥasan narrated by ad-Daraqutni and others]

عَنْ أَبِي الْعَبَّاسِ سَهْلِ بْنِ سَعْدٍ السَّاعِدِيّ رَضِيَ اللهُ عَنْهُ قَالَ:

جَاءَ رَجُلٌ إِلَى النَّبِيّ صلى الله عليه وسلم فَقَالَ: يَا رَسُولَ اللهِ! دُلَّنِي عَلَى عَمَلٍ

إِذَا عَمِلْتُهُ أَحَبَّنِي اللهُ وَأَحَبَّنِي النَّاسُ؛ فَقَالَ: "ازْهَدْ فِي الدُّنْيَا يُحِبَّك اللهُ،

وَازْهَدْ فِيمَا عِنْدَ النَّاسِ يُحِبَّك النَّاسُ".

[حديث حسن، رَوَاهُ ابْنُ مَاجَهْ، وَغَيْرُهُ بِأَسَانِيدَ حَسَنَةٍ.].

I. The First Translation

On the authority of Sahl bin Sa'ad al-Sa'idi (may Allah be
pleased with him) who said:

A man came to the Prophet (peace be upon him) and said: "O
Messenger of Allah, direct me to an act which, if I do it, [will
cause] Allah to love me and the people to love me." So he
(peace be upon him) said, "Renounce the world and Allah will
love you, and renounce what people possess and the people
will love you."

[Related by Ibn Majah]

II. The Second Translation

Sahl ibn Sa`d As-Saa`idi, may Allaah be pleased with him,
said that a man approached the Prophet, sallallaahu `alayhi
wa sallam, and said:

"O Allaah's Messenger, guide me to an action which, if I do it, Allaah will Love me, and people will love me." Allaah's Messenger, sallallaahu ʿalayhi wa sallam, replied: "Be an ascetic in this world, and Allaah the Exalted will Love you, and be an ascetic regarding what is in the hands of the people, and the people will love you."

[Reported by Ibn Maajah (4102)]

III. The Third Translation

On the authority of Abul-ʿAbbās, Sahl bin Saʿd as-Sāʿidi, who said: A man came to the Prophet (ﷺ) and said : "O Messenger of Allah, direct me to a deed which, when I have done it, Allah will love me and people will love me."

So he said, "Be indifferent toward [pleasures of] the world and Allah will love you, and be indifferent toward what people have and people will love you."

[Ḥadīth ḥasan narrated by Ibn Mājah and others with good chains of narrators]

Hadeeth: 32 :الحديث

عَنْ أَبِي سَعِيدٍ سَعْدِ بْنِ مَالِكِ بْنِ سِنَانٍ الْخُدْرِيّ رَضِيَ اللهُ عَنْهُ أَنَّ رَسُولَ اللهِ

صلى الله عليه وسلم قَالَ:

" لَا ضَرَرَ وَلَا ضِرَارَ".

[حَدِيثٌ حَسَنٌ، رَوَاهُ ابْنُ مَاجَهْ، وَالدَّارَقُطْنِيّ، وَغَيْرُهُمَا.]

I.   The First Translation

It was related on the authority of Abu Sa'id Sa'd bin Malik
bin Sinan al-Khudri (may Allah be pleased with him) that the
Messenger of Allah (peace be upon him) said:

There should be neither harming nor reciprocating harm.

[A excellent hadith which Ibn Majah, Al-Daraqutni and others]

II. The Second Translation

Abu Sa`eed Al-Khudri, may Allaah be pleased with him,
reported that the Prophet, sallallaahu `alayhi wa sallam, said:

"There should be neither harming [Dharar] nor reciprocating
harm [Dhiraar]."

[Reported by Ibn Maajah, Ad-Daaraqutni, and others]

III. The Third Translation

On the authority of Abū Sa`eed, Sa`d bin Mālik bin Sinān
al-Khudri, that the Messenger of Allah (ﷺ) said:

"Let there be no harm [to anyone] and no harming [in
reciprocation]."

[Ḥadīth ḥasan narrated by Ibn Mājah, ad-Daraqutni and others]

Hadeeth: 33 :الحديث

عَنْ ابْنِ عَبَّاسٍ رَضِيَ اللّٰهُ عَنْهُمَا أَنَّ رَسُولَ اللّٰهِ صلى الله عليه وسلم قَالَ:
"لَوْ يُعْطَى النَّاسُ بِدَعْوَاهُمْ لَادَّعَى رِجَالٌ أَمْوَالَ قَوْمٍ وَدِمَاءَهُمْ، لَكِنَّ الْبَيِّنَةَ
عَلَى الْمُدَّعِي، وَالْيَمِينَ عَلَى مَنْ أَنْكَرَ".

[حَدِيثٌ حَسَنٌ، رَوَاهُ الْبَيْهَقِيّ فِي "السنن"، وَغَيْرُهُ]

I. The First Translation

On the authority of Ibn Abbas (may Allah be pleased with him), that the Messenger of Allah (peace be upon him) said:

Were people to be given everything that they claimed, men would [unjustly] claim the wealth and lives of [other] people. But, the onus of proof is upon the claimant, and the taking of an oath is upon him who denies.

[Related by Baihaqi]

II. The Second Translation

Ibn ʿAbbaas, may Allaah be pleased with him, reported that the Messenger of Allaah, sallallaahu ʿalayhi wa sallam, said:

"If people were to be given merely because of their claim, people would claim the right to the wealth and blood of others. However, the burden of proof is on the claimant and the right hand oath is incumbent on the one who denies it."

[reported by Al-Bayhaqi and others]

III. The Third Translation

On the authority of Ibn ʿAbbās that the Messenger of Allah
(ﷺ) said:

"If people were given according to their claim, men would have
laid claim to the properties of [another] people as well as their
blood; but the [burden of] proof is on the claimant, and the
oath is [incumbent] on him who denies."

[Ḥadīth ḥasan narrated by al-Bayhaqi and others]

عَنْ أَبِي سَعِيدٍ الْخُدْرِيّ رَضِيَ اللهُ عَنْهُ قَالَ سَمِعْت رَسُولَ اللّهِ صلى الله عليه وسلم يَقُولُ:

"مَنْ رَأَى مِنْكُمْ مُنْكَرًا فَلْيُغَيِّرْهُ بِيَدِهِ، فَإِنْ لَمْ يَسْتَطِعْ فَبِلِسَانِهِ، فَإِنْ لَمْ يَسْتَطِعْ فَبِقَلْبِهِ، وَذَلِكَ أَضْعَفُ الْإِيمَانِ".

رَوَاهُ: [مُسْلِمٌ].

I.   The First Translation

On the authority of Abu Sa'eed al-Khudree (may Allah be pleased with him) who said: I heard the Messenger of Allah (saw) say,

"Whoso- ever of you sees an evil, let him change it with his hand; and if he is not able to do so, then [let him change it] with his tongue; and if he is not able to do so, then with his heart — and that is the weakest of faith."

[Related by Muslim]

II. The Second Translation

Abu Sa`eed Al-Khudri, may Allaah be pleased with him, reported that Allaah's Messenger, sallallaahu `alayhi wa sallam, said:

"If one of you sees something reprehensible, they should

change it with their hand, if they cannot, then with their tongue, and if they cannot, then with their heart, and that is the weakest of faith."

[Reported by Muslim (49).]

III. The Third Translation

On the authority of Abū Saʿeed al-Khudri, who said: I heard the Messenger of Allah (ﷺ) say:

"Whoever of you sees a wrong – let him change it by his hand; and if he is not able, then with his tongue; and if he is not able, then with his heart – and that is the weakest of faith."

[Narrated by Muslim]

عَنْ أَبِي هُرَيْرَةَ رَضِيَ اللهُ عَنْهُ قَالَ:

قَالَ رَسُولُ اللَّهِ صلى الله عليه وسلم " لَا تَحَاسَدُوا، وَلَا تَنَاجَشُوا، وَلَا تَبَاغَضُوا، وَلَا تَدَابَرُوا، وَلَا يَبِعْ بَعْضُكُمْ عَلَى بَيْعِ بَعْضٍ، وَكُونُوا عِبَادَ اللَّهِ إِخْوَانًا، الْمُسْلِمُ أَخُو الْمُسْلِمِ، لَا يَظْلِمُهُ، وَلَا يَخْذُلُهُ، وَلَا يَكْذِبُهُ، وَلَا يَحْقِرُهُ، التَّقْوَى هَاهُنَا، وَيُشِيرُ إِلَى صَدْرِهِ ثَلَاثَ مَرَّاتٍ، بِحَسْبِ امْرِئٍ مِنَ الشَّرِّ أَنْ يَحْقِرَ أَخَاهُ الْمُسْلِمَ، كُلُّ الْمُسْلِمِ عَلَى الْمُسْلِمِ حَرَامٌ: دَمُهُ وَمَالُهُ وَعِرْضُهُ " .

رَوَاهُ: [مُسْلِمٌ].

I.   The First Translation

On the authority of Abu Hurayrah (may Allah be pleased with him) who said:

The Messenger of Allah (saw) said, "Do not envy one another, and do not inflate prices for one another, and do not hate one another, and do not turn away from one another, and do not undercut one another in trade, but [rather] be slaves of Allah and brothers [amongst yourselves]. A Muslim is the brother of a Muslim: he does not oppress him, nor does he fail him, nor does he lie to him, nor does he hold him in contempt. Taqwa (piety) is right here [and he pointed to his chest three times]. It is evil enough for a man to hold his brother Muslim in contempt. The whole of a Muslim is inviolable for another Muslim: his blood, his property, and his honour."

[Related by Muslim]

II. The Second Translation

Abu Hurayrah, may Allaah be pleased with him, reported that Allaah's Messenger, sallallaahu `alayhi wa sallam, said:

"Do not be envious of one another, do not inflate prices on one another, do not carry mutual hate for one another, do not turn away from one another, do not engage in selling to harm one another, and be as fellow brothers, O slaves of Allaah. The Muslim is the brother of the Muslim; they should not oppress them, fail them, lie to them, or belittle them. Taqwa is here – and he, sallallaahu `alayhi wa sallam, pointed to his heart three times – it is enough evil for a person to belittle their Muslim brother or Muslim. Everything of a Muslim is sacred to the Muslim, including their blood, wealth, and honor."

[Reported by Muslim (2564).]

III. The Third Translation

On the authority of Abū Hurayrah, who said: The Messenger of Allah (ﷺ) said:

"Do not envy one another; do not deceive one another in

bidding; do not hate one another; do not turn your backs on one another; and do not intrude on the transactions of one another, but be, O servants of Allah, brothers. A Muslim is the brother of a Muslim: he neither oppresses him nor abandons him; he neither lies to him nor looks down on him. Righteousness is right here – and he pointed to his breast three times. It is sufficient evil for a person to look down upon his brother Muslim. The whole of a Muslim to another Muslim is inviolable: his blood, his property and his honor."

[Narrated by Muslim]

عَنْ أَبِي هُرَيْرَةَ رَضِيَ اللهُ عَنْهُ عَنِ النَّبِيِّ صلى الله عليه وسلم قَالَ:
"مَنْ نَفَّسَ عَنْ مُؤْمِنٍ كُرْبَةً مِنْ كُرَبِ الدُّنْيَا نَفَّسَ اللهُ عَنْهُ كُرْبَةً مِنْ كُرَبِ
يَوْمِ الْقِيَامَةِ، وَمَنْ يَسَّرَ عَلَى مُعْسِرٍ، يَسَّرَ اللهُ عَلَيْهِ فِي الدُّنْيَا وَالْآخِرَةِ، وَمَنْ
سَتَرَ مُسْلِمًا سَتَرَهُ اللهُ فِي الدُّنْيَا وَالْآخِرَةِ ، وَاللهُ فِي عَوْنِ الْعَبْدِ مَا كَانَ الْعَبْدُ
فِي عَوْنِ أَخِيهِ، وَمَنْ سَلَكَ طَرِيقًا يَلْتَمِسُ فِيهِ عِلْمًا سَهَّلَ اللهُ لَهُ بِهِ طَرِيقًا إِلَى
الْجَنَّةِ، وَمَا اجْتَمَعَ قَوْمٌ فِي بَيْتٍ مِنْ بُيُوتِ اللهِ يَتْلُونَ كِتَابَ اللهِ، وَيَتَدَارَسُونَهُ
فِيمَا بَيْنَهُمْ؛ إِلَّا نَزَلَتْ عَلَيْهِمُ السَّكِينَةُ، وَغَشِيَتْهُمُ الرَّحْمَةُ، وَ حَفَّتْهُمُ
الْمَلَائِكَةُ، وَذَكَرَهُمُ اللهُ فِيمَنْ عِنْدَهُ، وَمَنْ أَبْطَأَ بِهِ عَمَلُهُ لَمْ يُسْرِعْ بِهِ نَسَبُهُ".
رَوَاهُ: [مُسْلِمٌ].

I.   The First Translation

On the authority of Abu Hurayrah (may Allah be pleased
with him), that the Prophet (peace be upon him) said:

Whoever removes a worldly grief from a believer, Allah will
remove from him one of the griefs of the Day of Resurrection.
And whoever alleviates the need of a needy person, Allah will
alleviate his needs in this world and the Hereafter. Whoever
shields [or hides the misdeeds of] a Muslim, Allah will shield
him in this world and the Hereafter. And Allah will aid His
slave so long as he aids his brother. And whoever follows a
path to seek knowledge therein, Allah will make easy for him

a path to Paradise. No people gather together in one of the Houses of Allah, reciting the Book of Allah and studying it among themselves, except that sakeenah (tranquility) descends upon them, and mercy envelops them, and the angels surround them, and Allah mentions them amongst those who are with Him. And whoever is slowed down by his actions, will not be hastened forward by his lineage.

[Related by Muslim]

II. The Second Translation

Abu Hurayrah, may Allaah be pleased with him, reported that Allaah's Messenger, sallallaahu 'alayhi wa sallam, said:

"Whoever relieves a believer of a distress of this life, Allaah the Exalted will relieve them of a distress of the Day of Resurrection. If someone facilitates for someone needy, Allaah the Exalted will facilitate for them in this life and the Hereafter. Whoever covers the faults of a Muslim, Allaah the Exalted will cover their faults in this life and the Hereafter. Allaah the Exalted will Aid the slave, as long as the slave aids their brother or sister. If someone takes a path of seeking knowledge, Allaah the Exalted will facilitate and ease a way to Paradise for them. Every time a group gather in one of the houses of Allaah, reciting the Book of Allaah the Exalted and engaging in mutual study of it, tranquility descends on them, mercy encompasses them, the angels surround them, and Allaah the Exalted will mention them with those with Him.

If someone is slowed by their actions, they will not speed up with their lineage."

[Reported by Muslim (2699).]

III. The Third Translation

On the authority of Abū Hurayrah that the Prophet (ﷺ) said:

"Whoever relieves a believer of a distress from the distresses of this world – Allah will relieve him of a distress from the distresses of the Day of Resurrection. And whoever facilitates [a matter] for one in financial difficulty – Allah will facilitate for him [matters] in this world and the Hereafter. And whoever covers [the fault of] a Muslim – Allah will cover his [faults] in this world and the Hereafter. Allah is in aid of [His] servant as long as the servant is in aid of his brother. And whoever follows a path seeking knowledge therein – Allah will facilitate for him a path to Paradise. No people assemble in one of the houses of Allah reciting the Book of Allah and studying it among themselves but that tranquility descends upon them, mercy envelops them, the angels surround them, and Allah mentions them among those with Him. And he whose deeds slow him down will not be accelerated by his lineage."

[Narrated by Muslim]

عَنِ ابْنِ عَبَّاسٍ رَضِيَ اللَّهُ عَنْهُمَا عَنْ رَسُولِ اللَّهِ صلى الله عليه وسلم فِيمَا
يَرْوِيهِ عَنْ رَبِّهِ تَبَارَكَ وَتَعَالَى، قَالَ:

"إِنَّ اللَّهَ كَتَبَ الْحَسَنَاتِ وَالسَّيِّئَاتِ، ثُمَّ بَيَّنَ ذَلِكَ، فَمَنْ هَمَّ بِحَسَنَةٍ فَلَمْ يَعْمَلْهَا
كَتَبَهَا اللَّهُ عِنْدَهُ حَسَنَةً كَامِلَةً، وَإِنْ هَمَّ بِهَا فَعَمِلَهَا كَتَبَهَا اللَّهُ عِنْدَهُ عَشْرَ
حَسَنَاتٍ إِلَى سَبْعِمِائَةِ ضِعْفٍ إِلَى أَضْعَافٍ كَثِيرَةٍ، وَإِنْ هَمَّ بِسَيِّئَةٍ فَلَمْ يَعْمَلْهَا
كَتَبَهَا اللَّهُ عِنْدَهُ حَسَنَةً كَامِلَةً، وَإِنْ هَمَّ بِهَا فَعَمِلَهَا كَتَبَهَا اللَّهُ سَيِّئَةً وَاحِدَةً".

رَوَاهُ: [الْبُخَارِيُّ] وَ [مُسْلِمٌ].

I. The First Translation

On the authority of Ibn Abbas (may Allah be pleased with
him), from the Messenger of Allah (peace and blessings of
Allah be upon him), from what he has related from his Lord:
Verily Allah ta'ala has written down the good deeds and the
evil deeds, and then explained it [by saying]:

"Whosoever intended to perform a good deed, but did not do
it, then Allah writes it down with Himself as a complete good
deed. And if he intended to perform it and then did perform
it, then Allah writes it down with Himself as from ten good
deeds up to seven hundred times, up to many times
multiplied. And if he intended to perform an evil deed, but
did not do it, then Allah writes it down with Himself as a

complete good deed. And if he intended it [i.e., the evil deed] and then performed it, then Allah writes it down as one evil deed."

[Related by al-Bukhari & Muslim]

II. The Second Translation

Ibn ʿAbbaas, may Allaah be pleased with him, reported that Allaah's Messenger, sallallaahu ʿalayhi wa sallam, said in reporting from His Lord the Exalted:

"Allaah the Exalted has written the good deeds and sins, and clarified them. If someone intends to do a good deed but does not do it, Allaah the Exalted writes a complete good deed for them, and if they do it, Allaah the Exalted will write it as ten good deeds, multiplied up to seven-hundred, to many more times. If someone intends to do a sin but does not, it will be written as a complete good deed. If they intend to do a sin and do it, Allaah the Exalted will write it as one sin."

[Reported by Al-Bukhaari and Muslim]

III. The Third Translation

On the authority of Ibn ʿAbbās from the Messenger of Allah (ﷺ) is that among the sayings he relates from his Lord (glorified and exalted be He) is that He said:

"Allah has registered the good deeds and the bad ones. Then

He clarified it, [saying], 'He who intended [to do] a good deed and did not do it – Allah writes it with Himself as a complete good deed; and if he intended it and did it – Allah writes it with Himself as ten good deeds up to seven hundred times or many times [over that]. And if he intended [to do] a bad deed and did not do it – Allah writes it with Himself as a complete good deed; but if he intended it and did it – Allah writes it as one bad deed.'"

[Narrated by al-Bukhāri and Muslim]

عَنْ أَبِي هُرَيْرَةَ رَضِيَ اللهُ عَنْهُ قَالَ:

قَالَ رَسُولُ اللهِ صلى الله عليه وسلم إِنَّ اللهَ تَعَالَى قَالَ: "مَنْ عَادَى لِي وَلِيًّا فَقَدْ آذَنْتُهُ بِالْحَرْبِ، وَمَا تَقَرَّبَ إِلَيَّ عَبْدِي بِشَيْءٍ أَحَبَّ إِلَيَّ مِمَّا افْتَرَضْتُهُ عَلَيْهِ، وَلَا يَزَالُ عَبْدِي يَتَقَرَّبُ إِلَيَّ بِالنَّوَافِلِ حَتَّى أُحِبَّهُ، فَإِذَا أَحْبَبْتُهُ كُنْتُ سَمْعَهُ الَّذِي يَسْمَعُ بِهِ، وَبَصَرَهُ الَّذِي يُبْصِرُ بِهِ، وَيَدَهُ الَّتِي يَبْطِشُ بِهَا، وَرِجْلَهُ الَّتِي يَمْشِي بِهَا، وَلَئِنْ سَأَلَنِي لَأُعْطِيَنَّهُ، وَلَئِنْ اسْتَعَاذَنِي لَأُعِيذَنَّهُ".

رَوَاهُ: [الْبُخَارِيُّ].

I.   The First Translation

On the authority of Abu Hurayrah (may Allah be pleased with him) who said:

The Messenger of Allah (saw) said, "Verily Allah ta'ala has said: 'Whosoever shows enmity to a wali (friend) of Mine, then I have declared war against him. And My servant does not draw near to Me with anything more loved to Me than the religious duties I have obligated upon him. And My servant continues to draw near to me with nafil (supererogatory) deeds until I Love him. When I Love him, I am his hearing with which he hears, and his sight with which he sees, and his hand with which he strikes, and his foot with which he walks. Were he to ask [something] of Me, I would surely give it to him; and were he to seek refuge with Me, I would surely grant him refuge."

[Related by al- Bukhari]

II. The Second Translation

Abu Hurayrah, may Allaah be pleased with him, reported that Allaah's Messenger, sallallaahu `alayhi wa sallam, said:

"Allaah Said: 'Whoever shows enmity to an ally [Waliyy] of mine, I declare war against them. My servant does not draw near to Me with anything more loved by Me than the religious duties I have obligated on them, and My servant continues to draw near to Me with voluntary actions until I love them. When I love them I am their hearing with which they hear, their sight with which they see, their hand with which they strike and their foot with which they walk. Were they to ask [something] of Me, I would surely give it to them, and were they to ask Me for refuge, I would surely grant them it. I do not hesitate about anything as much as I hesitate about [seizing] the soul of My faithful servant: they hate death and I hate hurting them.'"

[Reported by Al-Bukhaari (6502)]

III. The Third Translation

On the authority of Abū Hurayrah, who said:

The Messenger of Allah (ﷺ) said: "Allah, the Exalted, has said, 'Whoever is an enemy to My loyal friend – on him I declare war. My servant does not draw near to Me with anything more loved by Me than what [religious obligations] I have imposed on him. And My servant continues to draw near to Me with additional works until I love him; and when I love him, I am his hearing with which he hears, his sight with which he sees, his hand with which he strikes, and his foot with which he walks. If he asked [something] of Me, I would surely give it to him; and if he sought refuge with Me, I would surely grant it to him.'"

[Narrated by al-Bukhāri]

الحديث: 39 Hadeeth: 39

عَنْ ابْنِ عَبَّاسٍ رَضِيَ اللَّهُ عَنْهُمَا أَنَّ رَسُولَ اللَّهِ صلى الله عليه وسلم قَالَ:

"إِنَّ اللَّهَ تَجَاوَزَ لِي عَنْ أُمَّتِي الْخَطَأَ وَالنِّسْيَانَ وَمَا اسْتُكْرِهُوا عَلَيْهِ"

[حَدِيثٌ حَسَنٌ، رَوَاهُ ابْنُ مَاجَهْ، وَالْبَيْهَقِيّ].

I.   The First Translation

On the authority of Ibn Abbas (may Allah be pleased with
him), the Messenger of Allah (peace be upon him) said:

Verily Allah has pardoned for me my ummah: their mistakes,
their forgetfulness, and that which they have been forced to
do under duress.

[Related by Ibn Majah]

II. The Second Translation

Ibn `Abbaas, may Allaah be pleased with him, reported that
Allaah's Messenger, sallallaahu `alayhi wa sallam, said:

"Allaah the Exalted has pardoned my Ummah for its
mistakes, forgetfulness, and things they were coerced into
doing."

[Reported by Ibn Maajah (2045) and Al-Bayhaqi (15094)]

III. The Third Translation

On the authority of Ibn 'Abbās that the Messenger of Allah (ﷺ) said:

"Allah has overlooked for me from my nation [what is done in] error and forgetfulness and what they are compelled to do."

[Hadīth ḥasan narrated by Ibn Mājah and al-Bayhaqi]

عَنْ ابْن عُمَرَ رَضِيَ اللّهُ عَنْهُمَا قَالَ: أَخَذَ رَسُولُ اللّهِ صلى الله عليه وسلم

بِمَنْكِبِي، وَقَالَ:

"كُنْ فِي الدُّنْيَا كَأَنَّك غَرِيبٌ أَوْ عَابِرُ سَبِيلٍ".

وَكَانَ ابْنُ عُمَرَ رَضِيَ اللّهُ عَنْهُمَا يَقُولُ:

إِذَا أَمْسَيْتَ فَلَا تَنْتَظِرْ الصَّبَاحَ، وَإِذَا أَصْبَحْتَ فَلَا تَنْتَظِرْ الْمَسَاءَ، وَخُذْ مِنْ

صِحَّتِك لِمَرَضِك، وَمِنْ حَيَاتِك لِمَوْتِك.

رَوَاهُ: [الْبُخَارِيُّ].

I. The First Translation

On the authority of Abdullah ibn Umar (may Allah be
pleased with him), who said:

The Messenger of Allah (saw) took me by the shoulder and
said,

"Be in this world as though you were a stranger or a wayfarer."

And Ibn Umar (may Allah be pleased with him) used to say,

"In the evening do not expect [to live until] the morning, and
in the morning do not expect [to live until] the evening. Take
[advantage of] your health before times of sickness, and [take
advantage of] your life before your death."

[Related by al- Bukhari]

II. The Second Translation

Ibn ʿUmar, may Allaah be pleased with him, said: "Allaah's Messenger, sallallaahu ʿalayhi wa sallam, took me by my shoulder and said:

'Be in this life as if you are a stranger or wayfarer.'

Ibn ʿUmar, may Allaah be pleased with him, used to say: "If you sleep, do not await the day, and if you wake, do not await the night. Take from your health for your sickness, and from your life for your death."

[Reported by Al-Bukhaari (6416)]

III. The Third Translation

On the authority of Ibn ʿUmar, who said: The Messenger of Allah (ﷺ) took me by the shoulder and said,

"Be in the world as though you were a stranger or a wayfarer."

And Ibn ʿUmar used to say, "When you have reached the evening, do not await the morning; and when you have reached morning, do not await the evening. Take from your health for your illness and from your life for your death."

[Narrated by al-Bukhāri]

عَنْ أَبِي مُحَمَّدٍ عَبْدِ اللهِ بْنِ عَمْرِو بْنِ الْعَاصِ رَضِيَ اللهُ عَنْهُمَا، قَالَ:

قَالَ رَسُولُ اللهِ صلى الله عليه وسلم "لَا يُؤْمِنُ أَحَدُكُمْ حَتَّى يَكُونَ هَوَاهُ

تَبَعًا لِمَا جِئْتُ بِهِ".

[حَدِيثٌ حَسَنٌ صَحِيحٌ، رَوَيْنَاهُ فِي كِتَابِ "الْحُجَّةِ" بِإِسْنَادٍ صَحِيحٍ.].

I.   The First Translation

On the authority of Abu Muhammad Abdullah bin 'Amr bin al-'Aas (may Allah be pleased with him) who said:

The Messenger of Allah (peace be upon him) said, "None of you [truly] believes until his desires are subservient to that which I have brought."

[Related by An-Nawawi in "Hujjah"]

II. The Second Translation

'Abdullaah ibn 'Amr ibn Al-'Aas, may Allaah be pleased with him, reported that Allaah's Messenger, sallallaahu 'alayhi wa sallam, said:

"One of you does not believe until their desires are in tune with what I have come with."

[An-Nawawi, may Allaah have mercy on him, said:
"This is an acceptably authentic Hadeeth, and we
have reported it in the book known as, 'Al-Hujjah,']

III. The Third Translation

On the authority of Abū Muḥammad, ʿAbdullāh the son of ʿAmr bin al-ʿAas, who said:

The Messenger of Allah (ﷺ) said: "None of you [truly] believes until his inclination is in accordance with what I have brought."

[A ḥasan-ṣaḥeeḥ ḥadīth transmitted
from Kitāb al-Ḥujjah]

عَنْ أَنَسِ بْنِ مَالِكٍ رَضِيَ اللهُ عَنْهُ قَالَ:

سَمِعْت رَسُولَ اللهِ صلى الله عليه وسلم يَقُولُ: قَالَ اللهُ تَعَالَى: "يَا ابْنَ آدَمَ! إِنَّكَ مَا دَعَوْتِنِي وَرَجَوْتِنِي غَفَرْتُ لَكَ عَلَى مَا كَانَ مِنْكَ وَلَا أُبَالِي، يَا ابْنَ آدَمَ! لَوْ بَلَغَتْ ذُنُوبُكَ عَنَانَ السَّمَاءِ ثُمَّ اسْتَغْفَرْتِنِي غَفَرْتُ لَكَ، يَا ابْنَ آدَمَ! إِنَّكَ لَوْ أَتَيْتِنِي بِقُرَابِ الْأَرْضِ خَطَايَا ثُمَّ لَقِيتِنِي لَا تُشْرِكُ بِي شَيْئًا لَأَتَيْتُكَ بِقُرَابِهَا مَغْفِرَةً".

رَوَاهُ: [التِّرْمِذِيُّ، وَقَالَ: حَدِيثٌ حَسَنٌ صَحِيحٌ].

I. The First Translation

On the authority of Anas (may Allah be pleased with him) who said:

I heard the Messenger of Allah (saw) say, "Allah the Almighty has said: 'O Son of Adam, as long as you invoke Me and ask of Me, I shall forgive you for what you have done, and I shall not mind. O Son of Adam, were your sins to reach the clouds of the sky and you then asked forgiveness from Me, I would forgive you. O Son of Adam, were you to come to Me with sins nearly as great as the Earth, and were you then to face Me, ascribing no partner to Me, I would bring you forgiveness nearly as great as it [too]."

[Related by Tirmidhi]

II. The Second Translation

Anas ibn Maalik, may Allaah be pleased with him, said that he heard Allaah's Messenger, sallallaahu `alayhi wa sallam, say:

"Allaah Said: 'O son of Aadam, as long as you invoke Me and ask of Me, I shall forgive you for what you have done, and I shall not mind. O son of Aadam, were your sins to reach the clouds of the sky and you then asked forgiveness from Me, I would forgive you. O son of Aadam, were you to come to Me with sins nearly as great as the Earth, and were you then to face Me, ascribing no partner to Me, I would bring you forgiveness nearly as great as it [too]."

[Reported by At-Tirmithi, and he ruled it as acceptable.]

III. The Third Translation

On the authority of Anas, who said:

I heard the Messenger of Allah (ﷺ) say: "Allah, the Exalted, has said, 'O son of Ādam, as long as you supplicate Me and implore Me, I will forgive for you whatever issued from you, and I will not mind. O son of Ādam, even if your sins reached the clouds of the sky and then you sought My forgiveness, I would forgive you. O son of Ādam, even if you come to Me with nearly the earth's capacity of sins and then meet Me without associating anything with Me, I will come to you with nearly its capacity of forgiveness.'

[Narrated by Muslim]